Ballyclare High School

The First One Hundred Years

Ballyclare High School
31 Rashee Road, Ballyclare,
Northern Ireland, BT39 9HJ.
Phone/fax: 028 9332 2244
www.ballyclarehigh.co.uk
email: info@ballyclarehigh.co.uk

Published in February 2004 by W&G Baird Ltd, Greystone Press, Caulside Drive, Antrim, Northern Ireland, BT41 2RS.

The quotations in the titles relating to Chapters 1 and 3 are from Miss E. Laird and Mr I. Stinson respectively. *Design:* Ms J. Thomson. *Back cover photograph:* Mr E. McKinney.

ISBN: 1 870157 58 3

Ballyclare High School

The First One Hundred Years

Kevin P. Conway

2004

I wish to thank my wife Claire for all the support she has given me and my two young children, Daniel and Anna, who provided not only a useful centre of gravity, but numerous periods in which to consider the school's history well beyond conventional working hours.

Contents

Foreword

The story revealed in this book is almost hard to believe.

A school, with its roots in a girls' 'finishing' school in a small County Antrim village, is bought over and moved to the local market town where, after a while, boys are also accepted. It grows to the extent where it receives Government support, then employs as its Principal an Englishman, who becomes the youngest Headmaster in the British Isles. Even after its third move, it soon mushrooms out of its new buildings and incorporates amongst its teaching facilities a Mortuary, or Rope Works as it is known, and a gas decontamination unit owned by the Ministry of Public Security, and all of this before expanding to a degree where more than half its pupils are taught in mobile classrooms. With further development it becomes established as one of the leading state schools in the United Kingdom, renowned for developing the talents of its 1,200 pupils.

For the details you must read Dr Kevin Conway's excellent memoir of Ballyclare High School: The First One Hundred Years.

Time and time again you will discover, behind the story of the buildings, a second story, of the school community advancing across generations with fortitude and commitment amongst governors, principals, teaching staff, ancillary staff and pupils.

Dr Conway demonstrates a school where partnership existed before it was fashionable, where mutual respect has been a key ingredient in its success, where a unique atmosphere has been generated and where excellence has been achieved through hard work and honesty, *industria et probitate.*

Robert M. McMillen
Chairman of the Board of Governors

Chapter 1

Small beginnings and "I hope it won't be foul weather for any of you"

No school has ever functioned in a vacuum. Schools have always been susceptible to the ebbs and flows of the world around them and, of course, a century ago the world was very different. The British Empire was well established, the United States had nearly completed its conquest for economic superiority, and Europe was hurtling along tight tramlines that would take it to the eruption of the Great War in 1914. It was a world of great privilege for a few and a mundane existence for most, where opportunity for social advancement was frequently frustrated, quite often by a limited educational experience. In the early twentieth century, the population of Ireland was well below the eight million souls alive in the doomed years before the catastrophe that was the Great Famine. The Famine had transformed not just the demographics of late nineteenth-century Ireland, but had also psychologically traumatised much of the island in what was an already tumultuous century. Some historians have stretched the parameters of chronology to call this the 'long nineteenth century'. It was born and ended with violence and unrest.

The 1798 rebellion fired the opening shots which of course, caught the attention of many in what is now Ballyclare High School's catchment area. The close could be many significant events, such as the outbreak of war in 1914, the Easter Rising, or Partition. Belfast had mushroomed into a large sprawling city that brought both the obvious employment benefits alongside dreadful poverty and the usual chronic public health problems. In 1800 the population of Belfast was around twenty thousand, but by 1900 this had increased to around a third of a million. The population of Ballyclare in 1904, when it became an Urban District, was just under three thousand. The pace of change in some ways was rapid. Educationally, the growth in the number of National Schools in Ireland between 1850 and 1900 was largely responsible for the fall in illiteracy. The 1890s helped usher in the age of the so-called Gaelic Revival, especially after the foundation of the Gaelic League in 1893. Indeed, the 1890s were also important in the government's policy of 'Killing Home Rule with Kindness'. It was in this decade, during which Charles Stewart Parnell descended into political oblivion, that it is possible to trace the embryonic origins of what eventually became Ballyclare High School.

The degree certificate of Elizabeth Dundee Adams Douglas from the Royal University of Ireland, 1892. *(The Ballyclare High School Archive)*

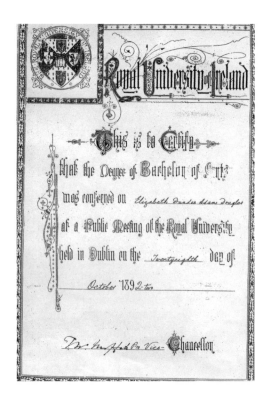

Home of the Misses Douglas' school, the Torrens Memorial Hall, Doagh. *(A. Reid Collection)*

Miss Catherine Aikin who assumed the role of Principal in 1902. *(T. Bennett and Sons)*

Many schools have a history that is both precise and accessible. For example, we know that the Royal Belfast Academical Institution laid its foundation stone on a rainy July 3rd 1810 and opened its doors, officially, at 1 p.m. on February 1st 1814. Belfast Royal Academy has roots stretching back even further, to 1785, when it opened on a site close to what is now St. Anne's Cathedral. Closer to the High School, Ballyclare Secondary opened comparatively recently, in 1961. However, the history of Ballyclare High School, especially in the very early years, is somewhat difficult to trace. The parentage of the school is clear, but unravelling the early chronological development of the school is not without its difficulties. We know that in the late nineteenth century, almost certainly 1890, two sisters, the Misses Douglas,

opened their school for 'Young Ladies' in Doagh. The school was housed in the Torrens Memorial Hall in the village. A decade or so later, the sisters wanted to close the school and sell the furnishings that went with it. This private, fee-paying school was taken over by Miss Catherine Aikin in September 1902. Florence Mary McDowell, in her portrait of life in the area, *Other Days Around Me*, wrote that the hall had been built as a memorial to James Torrens, who had been the agent to the Marquis of Donegal. She noted it was also called the school for "social climbers where for one pound per quarter, the children of the more pretentious parents learned English, French, Latin, Algebra and Superiority".

10

This photograph from *c.* 1900 shows the Market Square in Ballyclare with Warwick's store indicated. Above this store was the location for Miss Aikin's first school in the town. *(J. McKinney Collection)*

Miss Aikin moved to premises in Ballyclare in 1904, with the help of some local gentlemen. They included the minister of Kilbride Presbyterian Church, the Rev. Robert Allison, who acted as a guarantor for the school to continue in Miss Aikin's sister's house at the north side of The Square in Ballyclare. Catherine Aikin, a native of Bangor, County Down, graduated from the Royal University of Ireland. She had begun her career at an endowed school in Bangor, before spending four years as Principal of Fonthill College in Great Malvern, England. When she moved what was very much 'her school' to The Square in Ballyclare, lessons were conducted in two upstairs rooms. She admitted both boys and girls and part of the school housed a preparatory department, where the infants' teacher was Miss Meta Warwick. The school was located above what is now the 'China Rendezvous' Restaurant, but was then Warwick's general store. Mary Tyrell (née Davidson), a former pupil, has provided a valuable insight into what it was like:

As would be expected in a school of its size, a personal eye was kept on each one of us and good manners might almost have been a subject on the curriculum. Though solid hard work was expected of us all, no one would have thought of going home without shaking hands with her and saying, "Good afternoon". Nor were the finishing touches neglected. We learned elocution in the drawing-room downstairs and dancing in the Orange Hall. A vivid recollection of being referred to as 'the girl in the crushed strawberry' makes one realise that uniformity of dress was no more encouraged than uniformity of mind.

The Rev. J.K. Elliott.
(*The Ballyclare High School Archive*)

The classrooms, though small, were warm and two, at least, commanded a fine view of The Square. The seats by the windows were much in demand on market days and, during the May Fair week, the strain of keeping one's attention within the four walls of the room was more than young flesh and blood could stand. During the midday break the boys mingled with the crowds at the hiring fairs and often succeeded in getting themselves engaged by a farmer, whose shilling they were just prevented from taking by the ringing of the bell for afternoon school. Though it is improbable that any of them ever took the money, there is no doubt that a shilling represented great wealth to us in those days. One's Saturday threepence had to be carefully budgeted and the more lasting quality of a penny-worth of butternuts from the tuck shop at the top of The Square weighed against the fleeting joys of a slider from Miss Service.

In his autobiography, *One Small Head*, Arthur Fowweather, who later would take over as Principal after Miss Aikin, noted that the early school was run on goodwill and was financially in an extremely precarious position:

Miss Aikin was a courageous woman, for she ran her private school in order to support her widowed sister with her six children. She got good results in her little school where she could charge fees whatever parents could be brought to pay, and where she could pay her teachers as much or, indeed, as little as they could be brought to accept, for there was neither salary scale nor pension scheme for grammar school teachers in those good old days.

The school that Mary Tyrrell joined had a considerable reputation:

This exclusive fee paying school was, we all knew, attended mainly by the sons and daughters of the local professional families: the doctors, the bank managers, the solicitors, the rectors, the ministers and all such. For a member of an ordinary local farming family to propose to attend was, one felt, bordering almost on the presumptuous.

At the same time, Ballyclare also had a preparatory school that was run by a Miss Blair. This was taken over by a Miss Taylor and in turn by Mr J.K. Elliott and Mr J. Patterson in 1916. John Elliott recalled, in 1944, that he and John Patterson "changed the aim of the school and gave a training for intermediate and commercial examinations". In 1916, at Miss Aikin's suggestion, the Aikin and Elliott-Patterson schools amalgamated, with Miss Aikin assuming the Headship of the enlarged school, which was named Ballyclare Intermediate School. John Patterson left soon after the amalgamation and went to Italy to study Music, before returning to Belfast to teach the subject. He also went on to become a well-known operatic tenor with the Carl Rosa Opera. John Elliott, born in Doagh, served as Vice-Principal in the school, as well as engaging in some part-time freelance journalism before leaving in 1925. He received a call to the ministry and became a student at Queen's University and Assembly's College, Belfast. After his studies, John Elliott started his ministry in 1929, at First Islandmagee Presbyterian Church.

Edie Laird, who had a long and distinguished teaching career at Ballyclare High School, was a former pupil of Miss Aikin. Her brother and sister attended the school when it was located in The Square. A few years before her death, she put together "some thoughts on the origins and developments" of the school:

The calendar told September 1916. I was ready for school, 'Miss Catherine Aikin's Private School'. The title sounds very grand and elite, but nothing so in reality. The accommodation was rented premises in Rashee Road/North End: five rooms in total at first floor level, above shops, and approached by a very narrow, very steep staircase. The accommodation had no frills: no school badge, no school uniform, basic, or less than basic in every way. However, Miss Aikin had seen an opportunity and a need.

Miss Aikin's school *c.* 1904.
(G.C.G. Millar Collection)

Miss Blair's school in 1903.
(Miss Blair is seated on the
far left of the photograph.)
*(The Ballyclare High School
Archive)*

Miss Taylor's school in 1916. (Miss Taylor is third from the right.)
(The Ballyclare High School Archive)

The school's new home in 1916 on the Rashee Road above what is now an opticians.
(*K. Conway Collection*)

Contemporary accounts of the school run by Miss Aikin effectively give us a flavour of what the experience of being at such an establishment was like in the early twentieth century. Lunch was apparently eaten in a small cloakroom landing at the head of the stairs. As mentioned earlier, there was no school uniform and interestingly, Mary Tyrrell noted:

Those were non-fashion conscious days. There we were, teenagers all, giving no critical thought or appraisal to what we or our companions wore. Whatever our mothers supplied to us we put on without question. Hair was never thought about and make-up was unknown to us.

M.L. Hay reflected on what it was like to attend the 'school above the shop':

Starting at Miss Aikin's was a great adventure to a little girl of eight years of age who had never been to school before. In my eyes there was nothing strange in going to school in rooms above two shops. It was all part of a day's fun to clatter up and down the flight of narrow steep stairs which led to the classrooms. It was a great game to throw someone's bag downstairs and watch him scramble for his things at the bottom. On either side of the stairs were the classrooms. Through the door to the right was the 'big room' and beyond it were two smaller rooms. These held the junior pupils of the school. At the top of the stairs, to the left, was a passage, off which were three rooms. The first was occupied by a music teacher, and the seniors in the next room read 'Julius Caesar' and translated the French poets to the accompaniment of scales, arpeggios and 'Home Sweet Home with variations'. Beyond the second room was that mystery of mysteries, the Chemistry laboratory. These badly-lit, badly-ventilated rooms, all with smoking chimneys, were the forerunners of what we are now proud to call Ballyclare High School.

The move to the first premises on the Rashee Road had been made in 1916. The school was located over what is now an optician's. Miss Aikin, in addition to being the school's Principal, taught English and French and did a full teaching week. Edie Laird recalled:

I suppose most, if not all, teachers have foibles: Miss Aikin wore pince-nez spectacles and these came off to be banged on her desk when her excitement waned. I can remember occasions when I helped to look for a missing lens and when it was found, watched as it was replaced in its frame. But there were never titters of amusement, such was our respect. Indeed, as I grew older, like many others I was sorry for Miss Aikin: she had responsibilities beyond school.

Edie Laird provided a similarly vivid description of the school:

The stairs leading to the classrooms were narrow and steep with no covering on the wood. There was only one straight flight, at the top of which a narrow corridor, to the left, led to the 'wee room' and off it was the 'Science Laboratory'. Also opening from this corridor, to the left, was Miss Brown's Music Room. Returning to the top of the stairs, a door led into the girls' cloakroom. Boys' apparel had to hang on pegs along the corridor just mentioned and off this diminutive cloakroom, the toilet. It baffles description: size about 3' by 2', lighted by a small skylight window and containing a long bench-like seat with accommodating circular hole and a receiving receptacle at ground level in a shed which housed bicycles. This contraption scared me. I was afraid that 'little me' would slip into Calcutta's Black Hole or somewhere far worse!

In the 'big room' three classes were positioned to give maximum privacy. Behind a large blackboard was the 'Business Section' where Miss Maybin taught Business Studies; Bookkeeping, Shorthand and Typing. The music of the good old-fashioned typewriter was a lovely accompaniment to lessons in History, French and English. Out of the 'Big Room', a door led into the middle room with an exit into the Preparatory Room where my education began.

Edie Laird noted that the 'big room':

… was our playground – there was no outside space at all – and as we romped we often caused chaos and damage to the bottles etc. on open shelves in two shops below: one was a pork store; the other a grocery shop. The former was owned by William Hill, a giant in stature and in girth. He often came up the stairs carrying broken bottles and, if the contents had been tomato sauce, his large hands looked gory. He frightened me. His approach was always announced by his bellow, "Where is Miss Aikin?"

Miss Aikin had never to be contacted. Hearing the commotion, she came from her room and, speaking in her quiet voice, she would say, "Now, Willie, come with me and we'll sort this out".

Poor Miss Aikin must have spent a fortune in compensation!

The school received its water supply from a pump across the street and so the pupils had regularly to carry supplies; sore shins were apparently very common. The school was heated by coal-burning fires, apart from the laboratory that was heated by a select number of bunsen burners. During the 1920s the teaching of Business Studies stopped and Miss Maybin was transferred to teach History and Geography. On April 7th 1924 the first edition of the school magazine appeared. Some editions may have been handwritten, although all copies seem to have descended into the mists of time.

Miss Aikin
Miss Shaw
Miss Maybin
Miss Wright (Preparatory)
Miss Sherrard
Miss McIlhatton
Mr Elliott

The teaching staff of Miss Aikin's school in 1924. This was also Mr J.K. Elliott's penultimate year with the school and the year before the arrival of the new Principal, Mr Arthur Fowweather.

Events beyond Ballyclare had serious implications for the school. In 1921 the new state of Northern Ireland was born with the Partition of the island. The newly-devolved government had made clear that the Ministry of Education would not give any grants to private schools. They would have to go into public ownership, if they could not sustain their financial independence. Fees would continue, but the whole structure governing the school was to be redefined. At a meeting held in the Orange Hall on July 9th 1923, Miss Aikin informed those present that, under the new Education Act for Secondary Education in Northern Ireland, all schools had to have a Board of Governors. After discussion, it was agreed to convene such a board and the Rev. William Brann, from the Parade Manse, Ballyeaston, was unanimously appointed the first

THIS INDENTURE made the 23rd day of July 1925 BETWEEN CATHERINE AIKIN B.A., of Ballyclare in the County of Antrim School Teacher of the one part and WILLIAM BRANN B.A., LL.B., of Ballyeaston Presbyterian Minister WILLIAM JOHN HARRISON of Ballyeaston Presbyterian Minister JEAN xx KILLEN M.A., of Holestone Married Woman KENNETH C. KIRK-PATRICK Lieutenant Royal Navy (retired) of Ballyclare xx Gentleman SAMUEL COLEMAN of Ballyclare Justice of the xx Peace and ROBERT S. THOMPSON of Ballyrobert Justice of the Peace and County Councillor all in the County of Antrim (hereinafter referred to as 'the Trustees') of the other part WHEREAS the said Catherine Aikin carried on a school in the Town of Ballyclare known as 'the Ballyclare Intermediate and Commercial School' and for the purposes of the said school acquired and used the buildings furniture and equipment and chattles specified in the Schedule hereto AND WHEREAS with the concurrence of the said Catherine Aikin the management and control of the said school has been recently taken over by the Trustees who have pursuant to the Regulations of the Ministry of Education xx

Document sealed on July 23rd 1925, showing the sale of the school by Miss Aikin and the transfer of authority to the Ministry of Education. *(PRONI ED/29/20)*

Chairman. At the next meeting, held in September that year, the Secretary was appointed, Rev. W.J. Guy Macbeth. As Edie Laird approached the senior end of the school, Miss Aikin retired and her replacement in terms of her teaching duties was Miss Muriel Brann. She was a daughter of the Chairman.

In 1925, what was known as Ballyclare Intermediate and Commercial School ceased to be a privately-owned school and was instead placed under the legal control of the Ministry of Education. This was formalised in an indenture made on July 23rd 1925. Miss Aikin was paid the princely sum of £96 for the school, and the premises and furnishings were placed into a trust to be managed under the auspices of a new Board of Governors.

These were momentous days for the school in so many ways. Three months earlier, at the Governors' meeting, a letter was read out from the *de facto* Vice-Principal J.K. Elliott, intimating that he wished to resign. At that same meeting, another letter was read out, this time from the Principal. Miss Aikin wished to resign as Headmistress but wanted to continue as the new principal's assistant. Reluctantly, the Board agreed to her request.

When Miss Aikin eventually retired from teaching completely in 1927, Mr Fowweather, who had succeeded her two years earlier, led generous tributes at the school's Prize Distribution and articulated deep regrets about her departure on behalf of the staff. The Head Boy, Thomas Dunlop, expressed regret at Miss Aikin's leaving and wished her well on behalf of the pupils. One of the Governors of the school, Mrs Jean Killen, read an official address at the proceedings. This is worth quoting at length, because it gives us a sense of the very deep affection and appreciation felt by so many towards someone who had an absolutely pivotal role in laying the foundations of what became Ballyclare High School:

It is with feelings of profound regret that your numerous friends heard that you had decided to retire from a profession in which you have long held a most honourable position, and, in doing so, to sever your connection with Ballyclare Intermediate School. We wish to take this opportunity to assure you of the interest and pride with which we have watched your work for education in this district.

In the secondary schools organised by you, first in Doagh, and later in Ballyclare, you not only directed the studies of a large number of young people, but you also bore the entire burden of management of these schools, being responsible for their financial organisation as well as for the purely scholastic department. We remember, with gratitude, that, having borne this responsibility for many years, you were able to hand over to the community a very flourishing secondary school.

We know that a teacher's work is mainly carried on through days and weeks of quiet endeavour, when often there seems to be no appreciable increase in knowledge, no great gain in character on the part of those taught, but as you look back now over the years you will name many who are valued citizens filling important offices, many who brought credit to their school by brilliant successes in public examinations and at the university. By your retirement, we know that the young people of this district are losing one who took a deep practical interest in all matters connected with education, one who was always eager to encourage her pupils to win success.

Miss Aikin then read a formal reply that concluded with the following words:

And now, with all my heart, I wish a bright, happy future and many years of prosperity to Ballyclare Intermediate School. My successor has at least one quality which I have been sadly lacking in of late years – that he is young, and consequently he has the vigour and energy of youth. He has an arduous task before him, that of at least starting a building fund for the erection of new buildings. This is no imaginary need; it is known to you all, and when, next summer, he makes a great effort in this direction, I do

trust you will give him all the sympathy and help possible. I would say to him what I have always felt myself: that the greatest happiness the heads of schools can have is when their pupils reach their objective and make a successful start in life. I am sure he will find it also. (Applause.)

Miss Aikin, speaking with emotion, noted that her chief feeling was one of sadness. After the vote of thanks, visitors were entertained to tea in the school by the Governors.

Arthur Fowweather took over in 1925 and, like Miss Aikin, he was a teaching Principal. Mr Fowweather was only 24 years old when he assumed the responsibility and Miss Aikin was well into her sixties. Educated at Bolton Secondary and Liverpool University, he taught Science and Mathematics. Edie Laird, who was taught by the new Principal, recalled how Miss Aikin told the school of his appointment: "I hope it won't be foul weather for any of you". Miss Laird recalled, "He was a bit fiery! And he was an Englishman in Northern Ireland. No comment!"

In *One Small Head*, Arthur Fowweather described vividly his first impressions of the Aikin school when he went for his interview for the Headship. The Governors were conferring in the 'Big Room' and Mr Fowweather waited for Miss Aikin to come to talk with him:

As I waited, fearful, stunned, nervous and curious, I looked about me. I saw that the two longer walls of this room were lined with what appeared to be some sort of antique lab benches with circular sinks set into them. I had never seen, I had never even heard of circular sinks in a lab before. They intrigued me. Waste pipes ran down from them and disappeared at floor level, but I could see no water taps. Everything was pervaded by the smell of dust and by a strong animal odour and a sort of feeling of fungus. Throughout my period in the building, an obligato of scales and arpeggios on a tinkling piano could be heard off-stage.

A. Fowweather – appointed Principal in 1925. *(The Ballyclare High School Archive)*

At the far end of the lab was an iron stove with a flue pipe that went up through the ceiling. Adjacent to the door by which we had entered was a tall cupboard of the kind I had learned to call a press. In the centre of this remarkable room were several old-fashioned desks to hold six pupils each. Their tops were carved to fretwork by generations of pupils in the past. Undoubtedly they had served the Misses Douglas well in their Ladies' School in Doagh. I was realising with dismay that I was really and truly looking at the school's lab. It wasn't a lab. It was a travesty. I promptly decided that I had wasted my time and money coming here at all. I simply could not accept such conditions. What a sorry place this Ballyclare must be to put up with this and sacrifice itself that its sons and daughters might come here. No, it definitely wasn't for me.

After talking to Miss Aikin, Mr Fowweather started to weaken somewhat and, partly due to the changes introduced to education after Partition, his remuneration would be noticeably larger than he had anticipated. When he eventually accepted the offer from the Board of Governors, he became the youngest principal in the British Isles.

Early in his Headship, it was obvious that the increase in enrolment had resulted in a shortage of staff, and at the Governors' quarterly meeting on September 14th 1925, it was agreed to appoint another teacher. The Principal, who attended the Governors' meeting in a consultative capacity, advised that, due to the number of boys attending, a male teacher should be appointed. This was not to be, and a female Mathematics teacher was appointed subject to approval by the Ministry of Education. Interestingly, at the Governors' meeting in November, it was resolved that "in the case of Ministers of Religion who have children attending the school, a fifty per cent reduction in fees be given, and in the case of teachers, full fees be charged".

During this era the school crest was designed. Samuel Douther, one of the school's first Governors, had two children attending Mr Fowweather's school. John Bell Douther and Agnes Elizabeth Douther, who incidentally was 'walked to school' by Edie Laird, played a crucial role in the design of the crest. Miss McIlhatton was teaching an Art class and asked John Bell Douther to sketch a school crest. When he was sketching at home with Agnes, his father noticed what they were doing and sent them to the Old Mill at Millvale to sketch the wheel and waterway. When Samuel Douther saw the sketch at home, he remarked that it looked good, took a pencil out of his top pocket and added the flax. James Warwick, a senior pupil, took the design and re-drew it as a potential school crest. In 1927, at the Distribution of Prizes, Mr Fowweather thanked the members of the Urban District Council for permitting the school to use their motto: *Industria et Probitate*.

In what was a comparatively small school, many former pupils remember a distinct sense of community. Some also recall the school song that was introduced by Mr Fowweather. It was called 'Play the Game' and perhaps shows all too well how things are very different in the modern educational dispensation:

Play the Game
Whatsoever in this life you have to do,
Play the game!
Always try to be above board, straight and true,
Play the game!
Though knaves engage in cunning,
They won't always make the running,
And if others choose to shuffle, why should you?
Play the game!

Chorus
Play the game! Play the game!
All true Britons do the same.
Win the goal by honest work,
Never sham and never shirk.
Play the game! Play the game! Play the game!

What was almost certainly the first ever hockey team at the school (1926/27), pictured with the new Principal, Mr Fowweather.
Back row:
S. Curry, T. Beggs, J. Warwick, J. Carroll, W.J. Stewart, G. McCullough and W.H. Gilmer.
Front row:
S. Stewart, T. Dunlop (Captain), T. Carroll and S. McKnight.
(The Ballyclare High School Archive)

Intermediate School,

BALLYCLARE

Headmaster: ARTHUR FOWWEATHER, M.Sc.

Assisted by a distinguished staff of Teachers.

Pupils are received from 6 years of age and are prepared in all subjects for the Junior and Senior Certificate Examinations conducted by the Ministry of Education for Northern Ireland—for the University, Banks, and the Civil Service.

Examinations for Entrance Scholarships held about end of June each year. Full particulars can be obtained from the Headmaster or Secy.

Prospectus with full particulars and list of recent Successes can be had on application.

An advertisement for pupils in 1927, from a Souvenir Book of a Sale of Work in Ballyclare Presbyterian Church. *(A. Reid Collection)*

The annual Distribution of Prizes affords us an interesting opportunity to peer into the events and activities at the school. Although this event is normally a time to recognise achievement, in 1927, as noted earlier, the downside was to mark officially the retirement of Miss Aikin. Mr Fowweather, speaking at Prize Night in the local Orange Hall, lamented once again the appalling state of the school buildings:

I am sorry we have not made much progress in this connection during the past year, but we hope soon to be in a better position for the teachers, pupils, and whole community are going to bestir themselves to collect money to form the nucleus of a fund for a new building.

The guest for the evening, Mr J.H. Robb, who was the Parliamentary Secretary to the Ministry of Education, echoed this concern. One of those present recorded the proceedings and the following extract is from an account of Mr Robb's address:

Like the Governors and the staff, he very much regretted, as representing the Ministry of Education, that the school was not properly housed. In that connection he might remind them that the Ministry had a double duty. It had not only to see that the instruction which was given to the pupils in the schools attained a reasonable standard, but it was also charged with the duty of seeing that the classes in every school were conducted under conditions conducive to the development of healthy bodies so that the instruction might be appreciated and attain its full value. The Ministry had been pressing, he hoped not unduly, upon the Governors of that school the desirability, perhaps even the necessity, of having better buildings and better equipment.

He was aware, of course, that the Governors had very much at heart the matter of the provision of better buildings. The lack of money was a root of much evil. He would like to commend to the general public and to Antrim County Council, for their most sympathetic consideration, the claims of Ballyclare Intermediate School for assistance in the provision and equipment of a proper school.

The Principal, of course, outlined the various academic successes of pupils at the school and gave the roll-call of those who had been entered for Junior and Senior Certificate examinations. He noted that there were 87 pupils on the roll, in the year for which he was presenting his second annual report:

The minimum period of attendance at a secondary school prescribed by the Ministry of Education was two years, and, as a preparatory year was highly desirable, it was clear that pupils should be sent to the secondary school if possible before they were 13 years of age. It made the work much easier for them and for the teachers if that were done.

Sporting success was also reported, especially in hockey with the mixed team unbeaten throughout the year. In what is another reflection of the inadequate facilities, Mr Fowweather also thanked the Rev. A. Holmes for allowing his grounds to be used for a tennis tournament. The objective? To raise money for the school library.

The academic standards in the school were very high and the school developed an enviable reputation for success in public examinations. Mr Fowweather noted in his memoirs:

When I had completed my first four years of Headmastering, 1925 to 1929, that is when I had completed my first run-through of Junior and Senior Certificate candidates. Out of that travesty of a Lab with its industrious Maths and Science, we had Edie Laird with First Place in Geometry in Northern Ireland, Catherine (Florrie) Gault with First Place in Geometry in the next year along with Second Place in Arithmetic and Third Place in Chemistry in the Province, and Ray Banford with Second Place in Chemistry.

As many associated with the school know, both Wilbert Hollinger and Arthur Fowweather have written in some detail about Scouting in Ballyclare. It is important to note that it was during Mr Fowweather's tenure in 1929 that Scouting began, and the school was used as the venue.

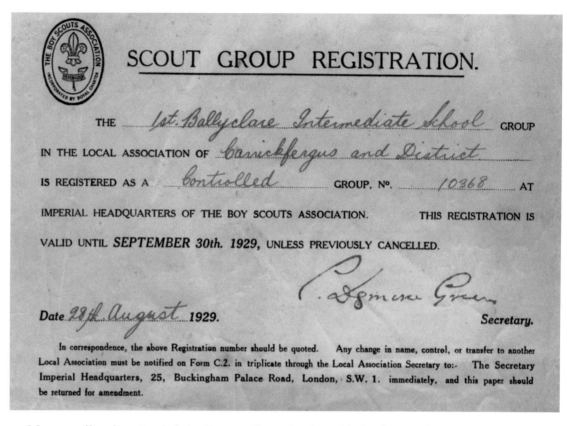

SCOUT GROUP REGISTRATION.

THE *1st. Ballyclare Intermediate School* GROUP

IN THE LOCAL ASSOCIATION OF *Carrickfergus and District*

IS REGISTERED AS A *Controlled* GROUP, Nº. *10368* AT

IMPERIAL HEADQUARTERS OF THE BOY SCOUTS ASSOCIATION.   THIS REGISTRATION IS

VALID UNTIL **SEPTEMBER 30th. 1929,** UNLESS PREVIOUSLY CANCELLED.

Date *28th August* 1929.   **Secretary.**

In correspondence, the above Registration number should be quoted.   Any change in name, control, or transfer to another Local Association must be notified on Form C.2. in triplicate through the Local Association Secretary to:-   The Secretary Imperial Headquarters, 25, Buckingham Palace Road, London, S.W. 1. immediately, and this paper should be returned for amendment.

(The Ballyclare High School Archive)

Many pupils who attended the Fowweather school, and indeed the Aikin school before it, had to walk a considerable distance. Some walked as far as three miles, to and from school each day. During the period when the school was located at the North End, the facilities were so poor that whilst the girls had a toilet of sorts at the top of the stairs, the boys did not. There was an entry behind the school. Sam Stewart, a pupil at the school in the late 1920s, recalled that the 'laboratory' was so sophisticated that the remains of experiments were put in a bucket that had to be carried down the street and emptied down a drain. Unsurprisingly, it was a priority of Mr Fowweather to secure new premises. In 1985 he recalled:

Form III 1929/30

Back row: D. Yorke, A. Magee, M. Harris, N. Wilson and L. Kerr. *Second back row:* J. Heral, F. Todd, S. Cody, L. Carmichael, I. Beggs, E. McKnight, M. Stirling and B. Elliott. *Second front row:* J. Wilson, A. Stewart, A. McCullough, S. Bamford, N. Douther and S. Ferguson. *Front row:* R. Howieson, B. Kennedy, W. Boyd, B. McCullough, J. Douther and T. Stewart. Taken in Mr William Hill's (Pork Merchant) Back Yard. (*R. Howieson Collection*)

… great work and all as we did in the Attics, I knew I could never rest until we had a building worthy of the pupils and parents of Ballyclare, to say nothing of the wonderful staff. One of the happiest days of my life was the day the first real Ballyclare High School opened in its smart new-smelling building.

A suitable site was given to the school on very generous grounds by a local trader, Mr Frank Lawson. He had been a tailor in the town and sold the school a site on the Rashee Road for £200. The ground rent was the princely sum of £5. Not long after his appointment as Principal, Mr Fowweather had learned that the school had an overdraft of over £800 – a huge amount in the 1920s - and several thousand pounds would be needed to purchase a site and build a new school. The battle for money from the Antrim Regional Education Committee was protracted and difficult. Representatives of the school had been sent to them by the Ministry of Education who seemed to be washing their hands of the problems over provision in Ballyclare. (Some might think that history had repeated itself decades later.) It is important to remember the context. Northern Ireland was not long established and the administration at the local level was suffering the inevitable teething problems of government. The Regional Committee told the school to raise some money themselves and then come back. Mr Fowweather noted that "someone suggested that the Governors and teachers put their hands in their own pockets. Willing and unwilling together produced £29". Eventually a Grand Bazaar was held over three days that raised over £700, including £84 from the sale of cakes, £158 from a refreshment tent and £13 from the sale of cookery books. Another application was made to the Antrim Regional Education Committee and they agreed to supply £4,500, if they could have two representatives on the school's Board of Governors. This was not a difficulty. After inviting tenders, the lowest was accepted and Hugh McLaughlin of Whitehouse commenced work after a bid of £5,000. The other seven bidders all notched up higher bids which were still less than £6,000.

BALLYCLARE INTERMEDIATE SCHOOL.

THE BOARD OF GOVERNORS OFFERS FOR COMPETITION THREE SENIOR SCHOLARSHIPS and ONE JUNIOR SCHOLARSHIP for the year 1929-30. Candidates for Senior Scholarships must be under 14 years of age on 1st of June, 1929, and for the Junior Scholarship under 12 years of age on 1st of June, 1929.

Entries, stating date of birth and School attended to be sent to undersigned on or before MONDAY, June 24th.

The Examination will be held in the School on June 27th, and 28th.

Further particulars on application.

ARTHUR FOWWEATHER, M.Sc.,

Headmaster.

An advertisement from the front page of the *Larne Times* relating to scholarships at Ballyclare Intermediate School. (*Larne Times*, June 22nd 1929)

Mr Fowweather noted:

The first sod was cut and what I came to know as the 'founds' were laid. I haunted the site, rushing up to it each afternoon as soon as school was over in the Attics to gloat over my palace rising from its rather swampy field. I believe I counted every brick that was laid. I shall certainly never forget the day I walked into the little room, with its adjoining private cloakroom with loo and washbasin, that was to be the Head's study and his own personal domain. I was similarly delirious when I could walk into a beautiful gleaming laboratory with taps that gushed water into sinks with waste pipes that actually worked and with Bunsen burners that flamed blue from the petrol-gas plant built under one of the lab benches.

BALLYCLARE INTERMEDIATE SCHOOL.

Headmaster—A. FOWWEATHER, M.Sc.

THE OPENING CEREMONY OF THE NEW SCHOOL BUILDINGS will be held on THURSDAY, 6th February, 1930, at 3 p.m.

The OPENING CEREMONY will be performed by VISCOUNTESS CHARLEMONT, and the OPENING ADDRESS delivered by the RT. HON. VISCOUNT CHARLEMONT, Minister of Education for Northern Ireland.

Chairman—JAS. L. CLARK, Esq., M.B.E.

Cards of Invitation can be had on application to the Secretary, Rev. W. J. Guy Macbeth, B.A., The Manse, Ballyclare.

Much discussion ensued amongst the Governors regarding the official opening of the new building. It was agreed that the Minister of Education, the Rt Hon. Viscount Charlemont, should be invited and, after his acceptance, advertisements were placed in the local press. Three hundred invitation cards were printed. As the ceremony was taking place in the depths of the Northern Ireland winter, the Governors approved the purchase of an item that generated a warm response from the teaching staff: an oil stove.

The new building was opened at its present site, 31 Rashee Road, on February 6th 1930 at 3 p.m. It consisted of one corridor with six rooms on the south side and two on the north side. There were a further two small rooms, one of which served as Mr Fowweather's office and the other as a staffroom. One member of staff recalled: "Utopia had been established". To state that the school had its shortcomings would be an understatement. It had no Assembly Hall, so two rooms which had a sliding door were used to create a venue of sorts. The Governors, in 1930, gave considerable thought to the erection of a bungalow for the Principal, and established an exploratory sub-committee to examine the possibilities. However, by September of that year, the Governors noted that it was "not in the interests of the school to build a subsidy bungalow" for teachers, including the Principal. Interestingly, the Governors paid the Principal £50 above what he was entitled to by the Ministry's regulations, at a time when the school was perpetually running a tight ship financially. Presumably, the Governors recognised that Mr Fowweather was delivering results and that the market in principals was very competitive.

Money was scarce and the Governors were meticulously trying to gain some additional funds from a plethora of different sources. For example, in the early 1930s, the school hired out its classrooms to facilitate elocution and dancing classes. Perhaps more importantly, teachers were hired for only a year at a time and each year the Governors wrote to them, with the exception of the Principal, informing them that their "engagement terminated" on a certain date, usually at the end of either June or July. Staff were

The new building at 31 Rashee Road. (*Ballyclare High School Archive*)

Sixth Form with Mr Fowweather *c.* 1930. Amongst those in the photograph are Jim Stevenson and Muriel Brann (back left and back third from left respectively) who both went on to teach in the school. Harry Coleman, sitting on Mr Fowweather's immediate left, was drowned in the Princess Victoria disaster on January 31st 1953.
(The Ballyclare High School Archive)

The victorious Ballyclare Intermediate School Hockey 1st XI 1931
Back left: E. Harson and W.J. McCullough. *Middle row:* Mr A. Fowweather, A. McConnell, J.G. Scott, W. Elliott and W. Boyd. *Front left:* J.W. Grange, H.W. Coleman, S. Stewart (Captain), J. Stevenson and W. Adamson. Mr Eddie Laird, a former pupil at the school in the late 1950s and early 1960s, who later taught Geography and History, recalled that his grandmother had to make shorts for William Adamson and one other player for the final. She bleached and dyed a flour bag from which the shorts were made at home. *(R. Clements)*

usually retained, of course, but there was no guarantee. Teachers were paid every three months, although the Principal was granted a monthly salary. Unsurprisingly, the wage bill of the teaching staff dominated the school's expenditure. For example, of expenditure of over £2,570 in 1933/34, teachers' salaries accounted for £1,665. This had grown considerably as the number of staff and pupils had risen throughout the 1920s and early 1930s. As far back as 1924, staff salaries accounted for only £1,137 and the Principal, Miss Aikin, was paid the same salary as three of her teachers.

This whole area of uncertainty over the permanence, or otherwise, of employment must have been disconcerting to say the least, but this was the reality of the situation at that time. A Copy of Notice given to teachers in 1924 still had a grain of truth in the early 1930s: "Owing to the uncertainty which at present exists with regard to the future of Secondary Education…the Governors give you formal notice that your present engagement with them terminates at the close of the current school year on Friday 4th July 1924". Perhaps this was a peculiarly Northern Irish independence day!

Mr Fowweather's sport was hockey and he had played for Belfast Y.M.C.A. The lack of room on the site prohibited the emergence, let alone development, of rugby so hockey was the mainstay of the school's sporting life. Success was not long in coming as Ballyclare won the Ulster Schools' Hockey Cup in both 1931 and 1935. One of the 1st XI players who triumphed in 1931 was James Stevenson. He had joined the school as a pupil in 1926 and returned as a teacher in 1956, eventually becoming Head of Mathematics and Senior Teacher.

The Governors first approved the compulsory wearing of gowns by teachers at their meeting on January 15th 1930 and it seems that some staff did not relish this development. At the quarterly meeting of the Governors in March 1930, it was "the unanimous instruction of the Board that the Secretary write to each teacher saying that the Board had agreed that they were to procure

gowns and wear them as from March 31st 1930". By June 1930 the war of attrition was nearly won as all but one member of staff was complying and the Chairman of the Governors raised this at the Governors' meeting. The female Preparatory teacher who was not complying was given "further instructions" that no exception would be made in her case.

The Governors on the January 28th 1931, discussed the question of having a photograph taken of the Board of Governors and the Secretary was to make arrangement for this to be done at the April meeting. Of course, the Governors became involved in many aspects of school administration. For example, in 1932 they had to give the go-ahead for the traditional Christmas social for the children and permit an extra day's holiday to mark the visit of the Prince of Wales to Northern Ireland.

Handing over the Schools' Cup at the Prize Distribution, December 1935. The Chairman of the Board of Governors, the Rev. W. Brann, is in the centre back with the guest of honour, Mrs J.L. Clark, receiving the trophy with Mr Fowweather looking on. *(R. Howieson Collection)*

A photograph of one of the earliest Board Of Governors 1931
Back left: R.H. Wilson, W. Loughran and J.S. Speers. *Middle row:* Rev. H.J. Osborne, S. McKnight, Rev. J. Armstrong, H. Gaston, H. Minford, Rev. A.M. Bell and Rev. W.J. Guy Macbeth (Secretary). *Front left:* Mrs Calvert, Mrs Ainley, Rev. W. Brann (Chairman), Miss Smyth and Mrs Macbeth. *(R. Clements)*

A priority of Mr Fowweather was to make his school better known among the educational establishment. The extent to which the school was operating in some obscurity was demonstrated when he met Mr A.R. Foster, the Principal of Belfast Royal Academy (B.R.A.), at a social occasion. When asked by the head of B.R.A. why he was not a member of the Ulster Headmasters' Association, Mr Fowweather replied that he had never heard of it. His colleague from B.R.A. told him: "We've never heard of you". In order to spruce up the school's image, Mr Fowweather proposed the introduction of a compulsory school uniform of red and navy with the use of a school shield. Last, but by no means least, the school name should change to Ballyclare High School.

As the school was now a controlled school, permission had to be granted by the Ministry of Education. Mr Fowweather wrote on behalf of the Governors to the Ministry. The change of name was agreed, with the Ministry granting approval, in a letter to the school dated December 22nd 1934. Of course, Ballyclare High School is certainly not alone in adopting its current name, years after its inception. For example, Ballymena Academy did not exist with this name before 1890, but we know that the school did function as the Diocesan School from early in the nineteenth century. Belfast Royal Academy did not receive the Royal designation from Queen Victoria until 1888.

By 1935 Ballyclare Intermediate School was no more. Mr Fowweather himself explained why Grammar was left out of the school's new name:

We finally ended up as Ballyclare High School, discarding Grammar as too imposing and redolent of grey stone, clock tower, shaven lawn. The other titles too were gradually thrown out as savouring of a kind of antiquity we did not possess. We were still an unpretentious redbrick rectangle with an unkempt hockey pitch. 'High School', being both unpretentious and of relatively modern birth, like us, became our name. This was not the only marvellous reform at this time. We teachers were now to be paid monthly instead of quarterly, and you can have no idea what a relief that was!

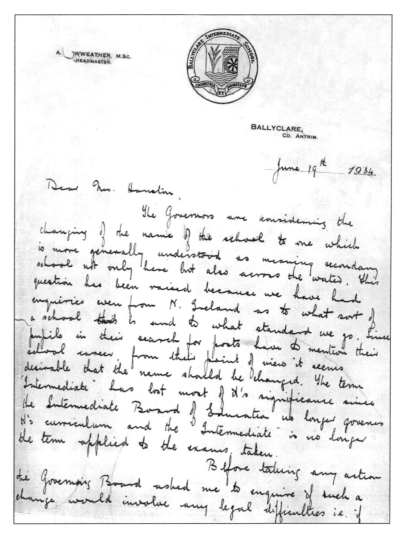

Arthur Fowweather's letter sent to W.A. Houston, Assistant Secretary at the Ministry of Education, requesting a change in the school's name. *(PRONI ED/29/20)*

S/8/2.   2 V December, 1934.

Sir,

In reply to your letter of 15th December, I am directed by the Minister of Education to inform you that the Ministry will not offer any objection to the change of name from Ballyclare Intermediate School to Ballyclare High School, which has been proposed by the Governing Body of the school.

For your information I am to quote the following paragraph from a letter which was sent to Mr. Fowweather some time ago in connection with this matter:-

"2. The trustees should, after the approval has been obtained, meet formally and pass the following resolution:-

'From and after this date the school shall cease to be called the "Ballyclare Intermediate and Commercial School" and shall henceforth be called ".........", and the Scheme of Management made on 23rd July, 1925, is hereby amended by substituting the words "....." for the words "Ballyclare Intermediate and Commercial School" in every case where the latter words occur in the said scheme and all reference to the school in the said scheme shall mean the school under the name hereby substituted'.

"3. At the meeting at which this resolution is passed the following words should be endorsed on the existing scheme:-

'From and after this date this Scheme is hereby amended by substituting the words ".....'' for the words "Ballyclare Intermediate and Commercial School" in every case where the latter words occur in the Scheme and all reference to the school in this Scheme shall mean the school under the name hereby substituted.'

The endorsement should then be executed and signed by the Trustees with their signatures witnessed.

"4. The scheme as so amended should then be submitted to the Ministry for formal sanction.

"5. After approval a certified copy of the scheme as amended should be forwarded to the Ministry for record purposes".

I am, Sir,
Your obedient Servant,

W. A. H.

Assistant Secretary.

Rev. W.G. Macbeth, B.A.,
The Manse,
Ballyclare,
CO. ANTRIM.

After resolving various legal hurdles, W.A. Houston replied to the school confirming approval for the name change. Number 2 displayed in the letter was passed formally by the school's trustees in the following year. *(PRONI ED/29/20)*

BALLYCLARE INTERMEDIATE AND COMMERCIAL SCHOOL.

ENDORSEMENT ON EXISTING SCHEME.

"From and after this date this Scheme is hereby amended by substituting the words "Ballyclare High School" for the words "BALLYCLARE INTERMEDIATE AND COMMERCIAL SCHOOL" in every case where the latter words occur in the Scheme and all reference to the school in this Scheme shall mean the school under the name hereby substituted."

Signed by us as Trustees this 28th day of June, 1935.

William Brann.
Teggee E. Speers   In presence of:-
Alexander McConnell
John Boyd
W.H. Loughran   *W.G. Guy Macbeth*

This amendment to the original scheme of management for Ballyclare Intermediate and Secondary School is formally approved by the Ministry of Education for Northern Ireland.

9th November 1935   *W.A. Houston*
                           Assistant Secretary

A document showing the signature of the school's trustees enacting legally the school's name change to Ballyclare High School. *(PRONI ED/29/20)*

Mr Fowweather fully appreciated that he had assumed the role of the school's public relations officer and that his relentless 60 hour weeks would not be consigned to the dustbin of history.

The involvement of past pupils is helpful for any school and Ballyclare High has benefited enormously from the hard toil of so many Old Ballyclarians. Record-keeping in the early twentieth century was unsurprisingly meticulous and Mr Fowweather relied on the many records of the school's past, which existed then, to assist him in locating former pupils. The idea of having an organisation for past pupils had been mooted as far back as 1930, when the Governors had discussed a request from Mr Fowweather to have their blessing for the creation of some sort of 'Old Pupils' Society'. The inaugural meeting was held on February 1st 1935 in the school. Mr Fowweather presided over the meeting that was attended by approximately 50 former pupils. The minutes of that first meeting record:

> the annual subscription for membership was fixed at two shillings and six pence with one year's attendance at the school as a qualification. The minimum age was also fixed at 17 years. That there was to be an Annual Reunion was decided by a unanimous vote and the election of officers would take place on such an occasion.

At that first meeting it was agreed that the President would research patterns and prices for a blazer and tie and, in addition, that "surplus funds from the activities of the association should be applied to the purchasing of sufficient ground to provide a full-sized hockey pitch and to the laying of a hard tennis court".

At the General Meeting of the O.B.A. on March 1st 1935 it was recorded that about 90 former pupils attended the first social meeting. What would become a long tradition of the 'Old Ballyclarians Formal Dance' was in the making. The first official 'Re-Union' was held in the school on January 2nd 1936, when over 50 members were present. At the social meeting on April 17th of

An extract from the minutes of the first meeting of the O.B.A., listing the names of those elected to office, with Mr Fowweather appointed the O.B.A.'s first President.

the same year, Mr Fowweather put on display a plain blue blazer with the school's badge on the pocket and the words 'Old Ballyclarians' inscribed in place of High School. A majority of those present approved of this design.

As the 1930s progressed, it became increasingly obvious that more buildings were required to facilitate more classes in Ballyclare High. By 1936 the school enrolment stood at 140. An

Old Ballyclarians' Association.

The Annual Re-Union

WILL BE HELD IN

THE SCHOOL

On Tuesday Evg., 3rd January, 1939

At 8 o'clock.

Subscription, One Shilling.

Arthur B. Cameron,
Secretary.

A G E N D A :

Secretary's Report.
Treasurer's Report.
Election of Officers.
Badminton Club.
Annual Dance and Informal Dances.
Proposal to alter date of Re-Union from Jany. to Sept.
General.

(The Ballyclare High School Archive)

exasperated Principal was having classes conducted in corridors and in the separate staffrooms. To help ease the problems, the Board of Governors bought 'The Hut', or 'The North End Hut'. This construction has assumed near mythical status in the school's folklore for many reasons, not least of which was the grandeur which it lacked. It was a prefabricated wooden shed that housed two classrooms. The total cost was £50, but it did help deal with a difficult situation.

A report by the Inspectorate for 1936/37 added weight to the Principal's complaints about the school's facilities. The extract below is given in some length because it provides a valuable insight into the problems and also because it provided a very substantial part of the overall inspection:

The temporary wooden structure with two compartments used for classrooms is crude, draughty, badly heated; in fact merely an uncomfortable shelter which could with better advantage be used as dressing rooms for games. They are most unsatisfactory for their present purpose. When it is remembered that the enrolment is 50% higher than it was four years ago, the inadequacy of the existing school premises becomes apparent.

There is a pressing need for an assembly hall fitted as a gymnasium. At present it is only possible to assemble the whole school by removing the partition dividing two classrooms and even then there is insufficient space. Moreover, this partition is very unsatisfactory and ineffective at best from an acoustic point of view. When a teacher on one side of it speaks loudly, it is almost impossible to hear the other teacher in the adjoining room. It should be removed and a permanent partition substituted. As far as Physical Training is concerned, it is essential to have a hall for the purpose. On many occasions the weather makes it impossible to conduct gymnastic classes in the open and then no attention can be paid to systematic physical development.

In one of the classrooms, preferably that used by the senior pupils, the library should be adequately accommodated. It is unworthy of the school to have this most important adjunct to complete education confined to a solitary bookcase in the passage.

There should be a room where the children, coming from surrounding districts, can have their lunch and prepare, if desired, a cup of tea or cocoa.

The school should either take steps to provide accommodation for Domestic Economy and Manual Instruction or an attempt should be made to induce the local Technical Committee, in determining on a site for the proposed new school, to locate it as near as possible to the High School so that the classes attending the Technical School for Manual Instruction and Domestic Economy might not lose so much time in going from one school to another.

The present state of the school building requires consideration. The ceiling and wall of one room are suffering badly from a leakage in the roof and parts of the ceiling in the passage are in a dangerous condition. The heating of the cloakrooms is inadequate, consisting of one small radiator in each. Many of the children have to travel long distances and must often be drenched. There is no hope of having their clothes dried under present arrangements. Attention is also drawn to the dusty and untidy appearance of some of the rooms which might be kept much cleaner.

Such were the problems of accommodation!

The Inspectorate did commend the general teaching quality in the school and noted that the teachers were "numerically adequate and fairly well qualified"! It did express concern, however, at the lack of subject specialists; for example, four staff shared the workload of teaching History in 1936. Four staff also taught English and the Inspectors were worried: "this arrangement is harmful by reason of the lack of effective co-ordination and progressive development which it entails". The Inspectors concluded that they had gained a "favourable impression of the steady effort on the part of the teachers and pupils … and that outdoor activities continue to occupy an important place in the life of the school".

With the obvious deficiencies in the permanent accommodation and the precarious wooden hut, Mr Fowweather broached the idea of an extension with the school governors. They gave their approval, somewhat nervously, because they were responsible for the finances of the school and the perennial overdraft. A delegation was sent to the Antrim Regional Education Committee, who agreed to an extension but, much to Mr Fowweather's frustration and disappointment, did not agree to take the financial responsibility for the daily running of the school.

During the negotiations with the Committee's architect, Mr Fowweather wanted to keep his hockey pitch sacrosanct and so the new extension, costing £8,000, joined the existing school at a right angle. What had become Ballyclare High School had gone from rooms above shops to a purpose-built two-storey building within a generation. The Duchess of Abercorn performed the official opening in October 1938. Perhaps ironically, it was during this same month that Arthur Fowweather first learned that Down High School was looking for a new Principal. He would leave Ballyclare the following year to take up this prestigious post.

Mr Fowweather's impending departure obviously had a significant impact on the Prize Distribution, which took place in early December 1938. In many ways this was a unique time for the school and the local community. With the rising spectre of Nazism in Europe, the school had its prize-giving in the brand new Assembly Hall at a time when its Principal was in his last year. Mr Fowweather informed the large audience that the school had introduced a House system to stimulate a healthy rivalry. One House was named after Miss Aikin for her seminal role in the school's early years, and the other was in honour of the Dixon family who had a long association with the school and indeed contributed generously to the prize list.

When Mr Fowweather assumed the Headship of Down High in January 1939, one of his first acts was to organise the inaugural meeting of a former pupils' association. Of course, it was no surprise when he became the first President of the Down Association. In the same year he also served as the new President of the Ulster Branch of the Irish Hockey Union, having been a member of the Ulster Council for many years.

1 The 1938 Extension.

2 A photograph from 1938 taken from what is now the Millennium Garden showing both the school from 1930 on the left and the extension of 1938.

3 A class working in the new 1938 extension taken just days before the official opening ceremony.

4 Governors, teachers, pupils and scouts await the arrival of the Duchess of Abercorn for the official opening. The North End Hut can be seen on the left of the photograph.

5 The arrival of the Duchess with Mr Fowweather and the Rev. W. Brann to her left.

6 Inspecting one of the new classrooms: Mr Fowweather, Lady Dixon, Mr J.H. Robb (Minister of Education), the Duchess of Abercorn and Sir Thomas Dixon.

Chapter 2

'R.E.', the Morgue and the unforgettable Sixties

Mr Robert Ernest Russell arrived in Ballyclare as Principal of the High School in 1939, just as Europe was becoming engulfed in another momentous conflict, barely twenty years after the 'war to end all wars'. R.E., as he was affectionately known, hailed from Dublin and had read Chemistry at the Royal College of Science, Ireland. He taught in Bangor Grammar for eleven years before coming to Ballyclare.

Mr Russell presented his first annual report in 1940, the headline from the *Whig* speaking volumes about the background in this key year: "Evacuation not allowed to interrupt school life". The wider scene was, of course, the Second World War. Its impact on the school was immediate and long-lasting. As early as 1940 the Governors had written to the Principal to stop the Scout and Guide camp at Magilligan that year and the 'Christmas Treat' for the children had been cancelled as far back as October 1939, with the funds being donated to the Ballyclare and Ballyeaston Soldiers' Comforts Fund. Mr Russell noted that the numbers at the school were double what they had been a decade earlier. The examination results continued to be impressive with 31 candidates entered for the Junior Certificate, of whom 26 passed, obtaining 46 distinctions and 58 credits. The school received a warm tribute

from the visiting speaker, perhaps nothing unusual, but the special guest in 1940 was the Permanent Secretary to the Department of Education, Mr R.S. Brownell. He said that he:

always thought Ballyclare High School was a striking example of what a country secondary school under their education system should be – a school where parents, governing body, local education authority, and staff all co-operated for the intellectual and cultural advancement of the pupils of the area.

R.E. Russell – appointed Principal in 1939.
(The Ballyclare High School Archive)

R.S. Brownell addressing the school during the distribution of prizes, 1940.
(The Ballyclare High School Archive)

Supper for former pupils in a
Chemistry Laboratory *c.* 1942.
Left: R.M. Armour,
Mr R. Campbell,
Mr R.E. Russell, E. Sloan,
D. Coleman, R. Howieson,
I. Beggs and B. Drennan.
(R. Howieson Collection)

At the Prize Distribution in 1942, tributes were paid to the Rev. William Brann who retired as the Chairman of the Board of Governors. Another House in the school's honours system was soon named in his honour. Mr Brann had exercised a guiding influence for nearly two decades, starting in 1923 when the school was taken over from Miss Aikin. Mr Russell told those present:

While a comparative newcomer to Ballyclare, I realise all that the school owes to Mr Brann's service throughout those years. Not only has he seen the school growing, but has in no small way been responsible for that growth from a school of 80 pupils in unsuitable accommodation of three rooms in part of a building to its present position of over 160 pupils in a building which bears comparison with any secondary school in the Province. We are happy to know that he remains with us as a member of the Board of Governors. I wish to thank Mr and Mrs Brann for their generous provision of two perpetual prizes.

Progress during the late 1930s and early 1940s was remarkable. Enrolment increased, as did staff appointments and extracurricular activities, while the reputation of the school spread in academic circles. Whereas Mr Fowweather had been the only male member of staff for much of his tenure, the school now had the Principal and Messrs Tommy Davidson, James Grainger, Bill Montgomery and Robert Campbell, who taught Latin, Physics, Latin and Mathematics respectively. The rise in enrolment produced severe problems of accommodation and so the now infamous 'huts' were erected. Quite appropriate in a way during the War was the nicknamed 'Big Three' of Messrs Grainger, Davidson and Montgomery. R.E and the afore-mentioned had a legendary interest in table tennis and it was usual for the team to practise at break and lunchtime. Practice was a reality at other times too!

Edie Laird, who returned to the school as a member of staff in 1946, gives us an insight into some of the staff around mid-century:

'R.E.' (Mr Russell) did not enjoy administering punishments so he left all such to Tommy (Davidson). He was quite expert and his expertise won him the nickname of 'Tapper'. Robert Campbell was 'Plum' and of course W.G. Montgomery was 'Monty'. Another was 'PA' – the owner of that was Mr P.A. Campbell who taught Biology. He was 'PA' in relation to age but he was full of youthful fun and tricks and at staff Christmas dinners or school parties we never knew what to expect so everything was treated with suspicion and caution. In spite of his trickery he was a gentleman, very popular with staff and pupils. Sammy Thompson who had been appointed to the English department was very volatile and his excitement could be intense. Sometimes, in the next room, his oratory could be appreciated, or otherwise.

Some of the staff in and around mid-century have gone down in folklore. Tommy 'Tapper' Davidson taught Latin, usually in the somewhat isolated Room 25. Prior to Tapper's arrival, discipline had been a concern in some Latin classes. This was to change. Tommy Davidson was a boxer of some repute and when he became

The 1st XI Hockey Team 1944

Back left: Mr Russell, M. Wilson, U. Shaw, V. McRoberts, J. Campbell and Miss Lusk. *Front left:* G. Graham, J. Bryson, S. Whittley, E. Graham, B. Finlay, J. Kirk and M. Erskine. *(M. Lindsay Collection)*

an assistant Scoutmaster he suggested that the boys should learn about the sport as well. They did and he usually tapped sparring partners in the face before the finale! Thus the nickname was born. The Scouts and pupils soon learnt that Tapper had been a middleweight champion at Queen's University. Respect in Latin classes ceased to be a difficulty. Indeed, Arthur Fowweather who had appointed 'Tapper' in 1932, described him as "a rock of strength". Inspectors, on a visit to the school at the end of the 1940s, described his lesson presentation as "direct and at times forceful". Former pupils recall that the jangling of keys or coins in his pocket was often a portent of impending doom.

Sammy Thompson, 'Sammy T' or 'Cathedral Sam', was undoubtedly another character during this era. Many former pupils recall with great affection 'Sammy T' and his vigorously enthusiastic approach. One noted:

Sammy Thompson was one of nature's gentlemen. He had a deep passion for his subject English, especially literature, but he had also a great knowledge of local history and the gift of transferring that feeling for the locality to his pupils. On a Saturday morning he would lead groups to places of interest on bicycle or by bus: the Moiley Bridge at Doagh on the old military road, the Norman Motte at Donegore and the Stone Age Cairns at Browndod all spring to mind. The bus journey to Comber followed by a long walk across the Causeways to Mahee Island and Nendrum Monastery in Strangford Lough was a real highlight for me. You can see how simple our pleasures were in those days!

'Sammy T' was a key figure in the organisation of drama in the school and many one-act plays were performed during the 1940s, such as *Elizabeth Refuses* and *The Bishop's Candlestick*. This complemented the expansion of musical opportunities in school, as Miss Catherine Lusk entered choirs in local musical competitions and music festivals. Indeed, the senior choir had won the Under-19 competition at the Larne Music Festival in 1947.

Prize Day in 1946 saw the return to the school of James Grainger who had been on 'loan to the government during the war'. At the Prize Distribution, the Head reported the success of past pupils, not least J.W. Dundee who did "exceptionally well in the fourth year medical examinations". Held in March 1946, with the end of the war still clear in everyone's minds, the ceremony included the reading of the Roll of Honour which included nine old boys who did not return from military service.

Despite considerable changes in the buildings, the staff and the number of pupils, a strong thread of continuity runs throughout the first century of the school's existence. A school magazine at the end of the 1940s mentioned something that would not be amiss in a publication from the early twenty-first century – "the Carol Service was held as usual at the end of the Christmas Term. To attend this service seems to have become part of the Christmas festivities in the town, and a large audience contributed generously to a most appropriate and worthy cause".

As the numbers expanded, the demands of feeding so many pupils were becoming a serious problem. The canteen had been established in September 1944 and during the next ten months it served over 22,000 meals. It is possible to understand why many connected to the school thought that improvements to the canteen had been long overdue. In 1948 it was noted that it was very difficult to feed so many "hungry mouths at midday". The canteen had not been designed to cope with an average of 250 meals per day. Inspectors were appalled during their visits in 1948 and 1949, that, at times the wooden dining-room was coping with 320 diners when the room was only meant to accommodate 100. Two sittings had to be organised and a classroom and the male staffroom were all utilised. Unsurprisingly, the Inspectors recorded officially that this arrangement was "most unsatisfactory and highly detrimental to the management and efficiency of the school".

The Kitchen and Dining Hall 1953.
(The Ballyclare High School Archive)

In what was a very different era, a member of staff in the dining hall had to ring a bell at the start of each session and say Grace in front of the assembled multitude. It was not unknown for pupils to burst into spontaneous applause on the days when 'Sammy T' was on duty. Grace would sometimes be multilingual and would embody post-war modernism as well as brief explorations into antiquity. This tradition of Grace continued until the old canteen was demolished to make way for the new school in the late 1980s.

If feeding the pupils was problematic, staff too had their grievances concerning tea and meals served in school. A deputation of staff, namely Mr Davidson, Mr Grainger, Mr Campbell, Miss Maybin and Miss Adair, attended a special meeting of the Board of Governors in October 1947 convened "to hear and consider complaints from the teaching staff". After negotiation, all sides apparently felt that the discussion had 'cleared the air' and a better understanding had been created between the Governors and the teaching staff.

The year 1948 was marked by the arrival of the school wireless. Some in Sixth Form explored the possibility of forming a debating society, but were put off by the impending examinations.

The school magazine noted in 1949 that "the growth of the school necessitated the holding of a separate Prize-giving Ceremony for the Preparatory Department". This was held on Wednesday March 23rd 1949. The Guest of Honour was the organiser of the BBC's 'Children's Hour', Miss Cicely Mathews. Music was provided by the children before the prizes were presented. The account in the school magazine recalled "choral items, short sketches, verse-speaking, recitations, and country dances made up a delightful programme, which concluded to the strains of a percussion band".

At the end of the 1940s the school's entire library consisted of about 250 books and the use of the term 'library' clouds another problem. Ballyclare High School had no official library as such and no reading room either. Clubs and societies sprouted up too after the war, some literally. For example, the Geography Club, Chess Club and Cacti Club soon attracted considerable attention. Sammy Thompson was the organiser of the Cacti Club and such was his enthusiasm that window sills in various parts of the school became, in the words of one his former colleagues, "desert landscapes".

School prefects for 1947/48

Back left: M. Taggart, A. McGuigan, R. McKinty, H. Boyd and J. McAdoo. *Middle left:* M. Kennedy, P. Wilson, Mr T.J. Davidson, J. Anderson and H. Bailie. *Front left:*
J. Houston, D. Moore, E. Kirkpatrick (Head Girl), Mr R. E. Russell, J. Leathem (Head Boy), H. Fee and J. Hill (Inset E. Robinson). *(The Ballyclare High School Archive)*

The late 1940s had ushered in huge change throughout the British Isles. The decade that brought the National Health Service also brought significant educational change to Northern Ireland, governed, of course, by a devolved administration at Stormont. The 1947 Education Act fuelled a huge rise in the numbers attending Ballyclare High School, with all of the attendant problems. In November 1945 the school had 244 pupils on its roll, but by October 1948 this had risen to 401 who were taught by 18 full-time staff. The Act was designed to introduce a qualifying examination for entry to grammar school at the age of 11. Schools were given direct grants from the government to cover basic school finance. This was the sort of financial assistance for which Arthur Fowweather longed, because a constant concern for him had been the ever-present overdraft and the fact that the school was very much responsible for its own budget. The 1947 Act resulted in the Governors agreeing to cede control to the Antrim Regional Education Committee in March 1950.

As the numbers of pupils increased, the High School's catchment area widened considerably. Records show that whereas the intake for much of the 1940s was dominated by pupils from Ballyclare and district, by the 1950s nearly half of the new pupils travelled from Glengormley, Carnmoney, Mossley, Rathcoole, Monkstown, Whiteabbey and Jordanstown. Indeed, in his speech in the Prize Distribution in 1947, Mr Russell expressed his thanks to the Transport Board for putting on a bus service for pupils attending the school from Antrim. Of course, rising numbers brought opportunities as well as challenges and the first girls' tennis team was formed in 1947.

Many with connections to Ballyclare High were keen for it to have its own rugby club. Hockey had been the mainstay of the school, but it was felt that "something needed to be done" to give rugby its place. The problems of inadequate or non-existent facilities are synonymous with schools in any period, but in Ballyclare the situation was dire. During Mr Fowweather's tenure the predominant sport had been hockey, not least because of a lack of space, but Mr Russell was determined to widen the range of opportunities available. A meeting of the Board of Governors on September 5th 1945 discussed problems over accommodation for travelling rugby players. (No-one would make the same complaint today, of course.) Mr Russell at that meeting stated:

Rugby players required a suitable place for washing after playing a match, and if the school could not provide such a place, then rugby would have to be dropped, as other schools would refuse to send teams to play.

A meeting was held in the school on Friday, May 20th 1949, with the Principal in the chair. Also present were Mr J.D. Williams, a teacher of History who would go on to succeed Mr Russell as Principal, and Mr W.G. Montgomery, a teacher of Latin, who also had a keen interest in the development of sport at the school. At the meeting Mr Russell stated that "suitable arrangements could be made for the club to have the use of the school pavilion and grounds". Ballyclare Rugby Football Club was founded that year and, at the A.G.M. in 1950, the name was changed to Ballyclare Rugby Club. R.E. was also heavily involved with Ballyclare Golf Club and had a most remarkable record as an office-holder. He served as Honorary Secretary from 1946-70, Captain in 1967 and President from 1974-77. His wife served as Lady Captain in 1950.

The Inspectors' Report in 1949 recorded that "the school has recently acquired a gas decontamination building erected on its premises, which is fitted with showers, lavatories, boiler, furnace, electric water-pump and light". This was the infamous cleansing station. This building belonged to the Ministry of Public Security, as did another building that has also gone down in the school's folklore, the 'Rope Works', or 'the Morgue' or 'Mortuary' as it was sometimes known. It had been erected during the Second World War, in case a similar building, off the Newtownards Road in East Belfast was demolished by the Blitz. An immediate problem

Kindergarten *c*. 1946
Back left: F. Hall, H. Taggart, B. Carmichael, B. Simmons, B. Logan, B. Ford and S. Hughes. *Middle left:* I. Murray, E. Ritchie, A. Chisholm, K. Lusk, M. Park, N. Perry, P. Campbell, M. Smith, N. McDowell and L. Baird. *Front left:* J. Finney, T. Noble, C. Milliken, D. Baird, H. Logan, S. Mairs, A. Rankin, H. Stevenson and J. Houston. *(H. Tempest)*

resulting from the construction of these buildings was that the school had to find a new playing-field. The Governors wrote to Ballyclare Urban District Council for rent due on the space occupied by the decontamination unit. They asked for £15 per annum; however, the Ministry of Public Security authorised the payment of only £5 per annum, so long as the unit was under the control of the Council. In later years, the whole edifice was to bring wide attention to the school when a pupil in the mid-1950s 'discovered' that it would have been used as a morgue for local people in the event of a German gas attack. A national newspaper reported the story and Ballyclare hit the headlines. After gathering the students in the Assembly Hall, the Principal and the Governors demanded that the informant be identified. This never happened.

It might seem implausible, but many classes were conducted in the distinctive surroundings of the Rope Works. One member of staff recalled: "It was a rectangular building, with no dividing partitions, only two 'cubby holes' at either end. No ceiling, just a zinc-covered roof, and an attempt at a heating system was abandoned. To reach this building from school meant a walk across an exposed plateau – no shelter from winds from any compass point". Therefore, it surprised no-one when the Inspectors, during their visit in 1949, lamented the poor state of the buildings:

The main building is in great need of internal and external maintenance. Woodwork and metalwork require painting to prevent deterioration, while some portions of the brickwork need to be re-plastered and others re-pointed. Externally the premises have an air of general neglect.

Attention is also drawn to the need for acquiring adequate and permanent playing fields. The present ones, which are inadequate and which require to be drained and levelled, are held on a five years' lease that expires in two years' time.

When the new rooms were added in 1938 they were furnished in a surprisingly meagre way. No seating was provided for the assembly hall, and teachers' desks and chairs, press

accommodation and office equipment were largely omitted. Only one clock, which is now out of order, was supplied so that reliance has to be placed on the antiquated method of ringing a handbell to signal the end of each period. Physics apparatus is still incomplete.

Further equipment required includes optical aids to teaching, a record player and records for Music, new desks for the rented rooms, blackboards, and apparatus for Geography, Chemistry and Physical Training.

Independent study in the senior forms is severely handicapped by the lack of a library and of an adequate collection of reference books for English, French and Science, of standard works of criticism and of interesting novels and journals in French.

An era began in 1949 when Mr Leslie Francey, Mr James Chesney, Mr Sam Bell and Mr Tommy Hooks were appointed. For many years they gave devoted service to the teaching of their subjects and to furthering the spirit of Ballyclare High School. Mr Francey and Mr Bell went on to become Vice-Principals and Mr Chesney had already risen to Senior Teacher before his untimely death in 1981.

Renowned local historian and former pupil and governor of the school, Jack McKinney, remembers Ballyclare High School in the 1950s:

I transferred to Ballyclare High School in 1952 from a small primary school and, with an enrolment of around 450, it seemed really massive to me.

Every term-time morning for six years I joined others from Cloughfern, Whiteabbey, and Mossley on the 156 Ballyclare via Mossley bus. What a motley collection of buildings met us at the High School! Other grammar schools had fine buildings named after distinguished former pupils. Among ours were the Rope Works, the Cleansing Station, the Orange Hall and the North End Hut. There was also a small Nissen hut beside the tennis courts, the command centre of the prefects, and outrageous were the rumours circling around the lower forms about what really took place in there. I didn't find out because I never joined their exalted ranks.

The staff, unlike some of the buildings, were far from old wrecks and, in my memory, most were young, lively and colourful. I remember them at their bases - gentle Mr Chesney and Mr Grainger in the Physics lab, Mr Bell amid bunsen burners and the smells of the Chemistry lab and Miss Lusk with her nymphs and shepherds coming away in the last room of the old building opposite the male staffroom. This tiny room deserves description. When all the male staff were present, there was hardly room for a cat. I know because I sometimes had to struggle in to fetch the cricket bag, which for some reason was kept in their loo. It was probably my imagination, but the cricket gear seemed to absorb a faint but distinct musky whiff from its unusual base.

The fairly recent prefabricated building had Mr Williams in Room 10 giving out his History prep and counting the school savings money, often at the same time. Mr Mudd in Room 11 read poetry in grave tones with his black gown swathed around him. Mr Sam Thompson taught English in Room 12 and, although volatile at times, was a very popular teacher. He often told stories of the cycling trips he made to churches and public buildings – a kind of Ulster Betjeman. It was a great treat to be asked to remain after school and help him unpack the new books from the boxes that came in from the County Library. This was the only library I remember in the school at this time. We were rewarded with sweeties, and an added bonus were the chips we bought on the way down to the late bus. Mr Thompson was also an enthusiastic Scout leader and looked fetching on parade in his corduroy shorts. This was not an unusual sight then, as all boys wore short trousers until around fourteen. He was by his own admission, a very indifferent umpire of school cricket matches. His attention tended to drift from the game to the hedgerow and the birds - 'the feathered variety' as he would have said with a loud guffaw. The cry of 'How's that?' would startle him and often his finger would shoot up nervously, irrespective of the validity of the claim. We bowlers well understood how to exploit home advantage.

Next to Mr Thompson were the French teachers, Messrs J. and S. Wilson in Rooms 13 and 14. I had Mr Jim Wilson and I remember his frustration, nay anger, at a classmate who after three years still pronounced the French definite article as 'lee'. The last room in this corridor was occupied by the lower forms of the Preparatory Department. The older children were taught in the Orange Hall and their teacher, Miss Ferguson, took lower grammar school forms for Nature Study. Her summer nature walks up Ross's Avenue allowed us welcome relief from King Billy.

Then there was the frail figure of Mrs Houston, our Art teacher. Her voice quivered and she loved elaborate lettering with lots of serifs. She looked 90, but was probably not a day over 70. It was rumoured that in winter she kept herself warm on the bus to school by sitting on a hot water bottle. All the pupils knew where she kept her handkerchief and it wasn't in her pocket!

Mr Cunningham took PE for a short spell of my time in the Assembly Hall and we changed for this, as we did for rugby and the girls for hockey, in separate rooms of the Cleansing Station. It was rudimentary and dark and suggested a military establishment.

Although Mr T. Davidson taught me Latin, my most vivid memory of him is from his supervisory duties in the canteen. Usually a silent threat, he commanded immediate attention when he gave tongue. No sergeant-major could have kept better order. Once, following a particularly strident bellow, I watched as his facial and throat muscles strained furiously to stop his teeth ejecting. He took tutorials in the smaller Rope Works rooms. One day, with three other boys, I enjoyed seeing Mr Davidson make several trips to the main door in response to loud hammering and shouting. This door stuck regularly but, on this occasion, the noise came from Mr S. Thompson. In an adjacent room, it turned out that he was giving his usual enthusiastic dramatisation of a line from the poem 'The Listeners': 'Is there anybody there?' said the traveller knocking on the moonlit door.'

We gathered from the tone of his muttering that Mr Davidson was not amused.

We had the 'Two Tommies' as caretakers. Tommy Rock was small in stature and genial – not unlike Ronnie Corbett – while

This photograph, from 1950, was taken by Archie Reid (using a small Brownie camera) when he was a pupil. A close friend of Mr Russell's son, he managed to capture the staff displaying something of relevance to their particular discipline. In the bottom left is Miss Maybin who was a stalwart of Miss Aikin's school, and in the front row on the far right is Miss Laird who recorded for future generations her thoughts on the development of the school as both pupil and teacher. In the middle row, the fourth from the right, is Mr Williams who would succeed Mr Russell as Principal, and the in the same row but fourth in from the left is Mr Mudd who became Acting Principal after Mr Williams' untimely death. *(A. Reid Collection)*

Two additional photographs taken by Archie Reid showing on the left Jim Wilson in his first year on his way to play in a Staff Versus Pupils match and 'Pop' Grainger off to teach a Science lesson. *(A. Reid Collection)*

Tommy Ferguson seemed to be permanently stationed outside the canteen, a cigarette glowing surreptitiously from his cupped hand. There was also another man in a white tunic who helped out exclusively in the canteen and was appropriately named 'Bones'.

While in the lower forms, instead of walking up to school, every Friday morning I went over to Ballyclare Technical School, to 'Stalag Luft Brownlee' for woodwork. This was an old ex-army hut heated like a sauna by a central pot-bellied coke stove, ideal for heating pots of strong smelling glue. Here Willie John Brownlee commanded a fine range of mallets and edge tools. With these, we produced elaborately jointed teapot stands and pipe and toothbrush holders. Well, mine were just about recognisable as such.

At lunch time the choice was either to stray with friends up the back lane beside the rugby pitch or play football. Here, there took place what my mother delicately used to call 'irregular gatherings' and, like her, I will leave their description to your memory or imagination. To Mr Montgomery's displeasure, football was played in the King George VI Coronation Field, just outside the school fence opposite Ballyclare Foundry. Despite its grand title, this was essentially derelict land with brown goalposts. It had been donated to Ballyclare Council around 1936 for public recreation, but never seemed to be in use. Later, in a deal between the Council and the education authority, the land was exchanged with the school pitches on Foundry Lane and provided convenient space for the expansion of the school site.

I have memories of many occasions and incidents when I was there. Often the annual Grange-McCluney Cross-Country Race brought an exciting finish to the spectators gathered at the final straight beside the Rope Works. In 1953 there were special sports to celebrate the Coronation in June and we received souvenir books and cups and saucers. I have mine to this day. The weather was beautiful. However, the most vivid memory occurred on the day when the school came close to evacuation. This was long before the days of bomb-scares, of course, and the cause was more mundane. The land on the northern boundary was still farmland at this time and the farmer chose a hot, still day to spread manure in this field. It was strong stuff and soon the smell went off the scale

The aluminium building in 1953. The beginnings of the 'huts' can be seen in the top right of the photograph. (*The Ballyclare High School Archive*)

on the 'sniffometer'. Complaints from the staff and pupils were long and loud and some girls and women teachers came close to being sick. However, fortitude in the face of adversity took us all through to half-past three and the performance was never repeated.

For me, the highlight of the year in the lower forms was the school Christmas parties. These were arranged in the evenings, a different night for each form group. Young teachers like Mr Hooks and Mr Francey joined in the fun and led the games. It was a rare chance to develop friendships begun in class time. Ten o'clock and the bus home came too soon and forced many sad partings. Those were the days!

Later the Old Ballyclarians' Saturday Night Hops were very popular as respectable alternatives to the wilder dances in the local halls.

An editorial in the school magazine in June 1950 highlighted the hopes for better accommodation:

A critic said of Jane Austen's novels that they contained "infinite riches in little rooms". The seemingly infinite riches contained by our school buildings have now burst their bounds and spilled over into that great vault known as the 'Rope Works Building', where four classes clutch at knowledge. Thus our hopes of new buildings have not been realised, although we have the definitive assurance that difficulties along the way have been smoothed over and that practical measures have been taken to relieve the acute accommodation problem.

The space between the Rope Works and the main school was being cleared in 1951 to make space for some 'new buildings', the huts. It was suggested at the time that perhaps the space was to house Ballyclare's answer to the London Exhibition, a feature of the Festival of Britain. Humour in adversity is always important.

To mark the school's great loss during the War, the Old Ballyclarians' Association organised the unveiling of a war memorial in the school on Tuesday, November 4th 1958. The service was conducted by the Rev. William Hall, from Ballynure

This photograph from the 1950s shows the Rope Works on the left and the edge of the North End Hut on the right.
(The Ballyclare High School Archive)

Another photograph from the 1950s showing the 'space' between the North End Hut on the left and Rope Works at the top.
(The Ballyclare High School Archive)

This photograph from the 1950s shows what is now the front car park and gymnasium with the North End Hut in the top right.
(The Ballyclare High School Archive)

An entrance to the infamous cleansing station.
(The Ballyclare High School Archive)

A Preparatory Concert *'Caledon Low'* from 1951.
Back row: B. Smith, D. Abernethy, P. Wood,
D. Simms, I. Blair, J. Hill, J. Wright, K. Bradley,
M. McVeigh, A. Rooney, R. Alexander,
M. Girvan, G. Parker, G. Buchanan and
B. Jenkins. *Front row:* P. McClelland, T. Howe,
F. McVeigh, H. Sharp, P. Robinson, Y. Rimmer,
C. Moore, E. McDowell and J. Murray.
(The Ballyclare High School Archive)

The school's scout troop with Sir Douglas
Savory on a visit to the Houses of Parliament
during the annual July camp in 1951.
(The Universal Pictorial Press Agency)

School prefects 1951/52

Top left: J. Magee, A. Reid, W. Rowney, D. Saunders and H. Logan. *Third row left:* J. Gillespie, J. Rock, C. Mackey, N. Simms, E. Greer, M. Hunter and P. Caughey. *Second row left:* I. Woodburn, I. Kerr, M. Patterson, M. Beck, A. Hughes, Mr T.J. Davidson, A. Marshall, A. McClelland, A. Woodburn, L. McGladdery and M. Coulter. *Front left:* O. Russell, H. Baird, R. Mahood (Head Girl), Mr R.E. Russell, R. McCready (Head Boy), J. Erskine and I. Webb. *(R. Clements Lyttle)*

Tennis 1952 *Back left:* Mr R.E. Russell, I. Black, J. Anderson, G. Brown, S. Stevenson and Mr J.D. Williams. *Front left:* J. Horner, A. McMeekin, M. Montgomery and M. Perry. *(R. Clements Lyttle)*

Mr Russell with His Excellency the Governor of Northern Ireland, Lord Wakehurst, with Lady Wakehurst, on their visit to the school in March 1956. *(R. Wilson)*

The cast of *A Midsummer Night's Dream* 1956 pictured at the front entrance of the school with Miss I. Green on the left and the director, Mr S. Thompson on the right. (V. Sinton)

An 'unofficial' photograph showing some of Form IV B and C (1956/57) outside the North End Hut at a break from football that was played on the rough stone of what is now George Avenue. *(K. Robinson)*

Form Upper 4 June 1956

Back left: M. Irwin, D. Ralston, W. Gamble, J. Wilson and W. Turkington. *Middle left:* D. Harvey, S. Steele, W. Cochrane, T. Andrew, D. Crawford, S. Rennison, J. McKinney and G. Bell. *Front left:* D. Wilson, M. Jenkins, G. Stewart, R. Dunlop, M. Cunningham, J. Murray and M. McMurtry. *(T. Andrew)*

Rectory, and Mr Russell read the names of the fallen. Miss A. Maybin, who had taught in the school from the Aikin era until 1955, unveiled the Memorial. This was also the year when the Badminton Club was formed and the Old Ballyclarians' Association purchased ground on the Doagh Road for use as school playing-fields. A couple of years earlier girls' hockey brought its first honour to the school when E. Kirkpatrick and I.A. Moore represented Ulster.

In 1958 the school invited Mr Alexander Keith, Principal of Stranmillis Training College, as its guest speaker at the Prize Distribution. The degree of frustration felt by Mr Russell as he spoke about the inadequate facilities at the school was obvious:

After presenting 18 Annual Reports it becomes difficult to present something new. It is unfortunate that circumstances are such that over the past 5 or 6 years conditions have not improved but rather worsened and consequently our work has had more than its fair share of disappointment and frustration. These conditions refer to many most unsatisfactory classrooms, to the complete lack of any form of playground, to unsuitable playing fields and changing facilities and to ridiculous staffroom accommodation. A number of years ago Ballyclare High School was a small school catering mainly for local children. The increase in transport, the growth in population and the large number of new houses in the surrounding area has completely altered the position held by our school. It is difficult to realise that since I came here in 1939, when there were only 150 pupils and 8 teachers in the school, the only additional new accommodation provided has been 6 classrooms and a canteen to cater for our present total of 560 pupils and 27 teachers apart from various temporary buildings. May this be the last report I make in which I have to refer to the conditions under which the pupils have to work and play.

The infamous 'huts' in the 1960s – stalwarts of school accommodation for over two decades, until the massive changes of the late 1980s. *(The Ballyclare High School Archive)*

The ever-popular annual Staff Versus Pupils hockey match. This photograph comes from the 1957 fixture. *(R. Howieson Collection)*

The Preparatory Percussion Band in 1958.
Back left: R. Thompson, J. Chambers, A. Robinson, S. Hall, D. Crangle, T. Kane, D. Corken, M. Davidson, L. McGruggan, M. Stewart, P. Gage, E. Stevenson, V. Finlay, B. Hunter and P. Caldwell. *Middle left:* I. Campbell, C. Bell, J. Holmes, G. Johnston, M. Bingham, J. Robb, C. McNeilly, V. Stevenson, V. Jenkins, E. Stevenson, O. Davison, Y. Connor and M. Montgomery. *Front left:* D. Simpson, R. Cooper, D. McNeilly, M. Montgomery, M. Swann, A. Mackey, R. Stevenson, B. Reid, A. McNeilly, P. Gage, R. McMillen, C. Stevenson and H. Grainger. *(The Ballyclare High School Archive)*

The War Memorial unveiled in the entrance hall in 1958.

Additional evidence of the wholly inadequate facilities was that the Prize Distribution in 1962 was held in the Assembly Hall of the new Intermediate School that became Ballyclare Secondary School.

In the same year D. McWhirter won the Northern Ireland Youth Cross-Country Championships and the school team was runner-up to Methodist College, Belfast. In the first year that D. McWhirter won the schools' cross-country race, one competitor had arranged for a bicycle to be left at the Cloughan stile. The intention had been to run the race after cycling down Cloughan Lane, the Doagh Road and Foundry Lane, but the competitor became unstuck when he found gates closed against him. Although highly placed, to the consternation of Mr W.G. Montgomery, he was not victorious. Some pupils had even placed bets prior to the race, but the outcome was not quite what they had anticipated.

Robert FitzPatrick, who would later become Principal, remembers vividly his interview and early impressions of the school:

I had been in Ballyclare twice in my life before being interviewed for a History/Geography post in the summer of 1960. This testing experience occurred in what was then Mr Russell's office at the end of the corridor, immediately on the right just past the toilet that was reputed to have been graced by the presence of the Duchess of Abercorn on the day of the opening of what is now called the Fowweather Building. I believe the Principal's office is now the medical inspection room, but in its chequered history it has also been Mrs Mary Williams and Mrs Hazel Topping's German room.

After a rapid tour of 'the school', i.e. the Fowweather building with the 'aluminium corridor' in which were situated rooms 10-15, the interview was conducted by Mr Russell, seated and just perceptible above the horizon of a large desk, and by the then Vice-Principal, TJ (Tommy) Davison, seated on the edge of the same desk, hand in pocket, as was usual. The warm welcome settled the nerves of the candidate, who only remembers talking about his

Form U4C 1960.
Back left: B. Wilson,
R. Cunningham, J. White,
G. Stewart, C. Bunce,
B. Neill, P. Kirkpatrick,
D. Crangle and D. Wilson.
Middle left: B. Ross,
W. Mundock, T. Hill,
B. McMeekin, P. Posnett,
H. Russell, M. Weston,
B. Curran, J. Burns and
W. Moore.
Front left: E. Meighan,
M. Beggs, S. Cummings,
L. Dickson, J. Robb and
R. McMaster.
*(The Ballyclare High
School Archive)*

interest in hockey and cricket. The interview could not have lasted more than 10 minutes and the point stressed by both of the interviewers was 'Would I take the job if it were offered?' I assured them I would be delighted to do so, little knowing at the time that I was the only applicant!

The school of 1960 was very different from that of today. The accommodation was totally unsuitable and many pupils have vivid memories of the Rope Works and the North End Hut. To teach in them was an even worse experience – how did one keep the class warm, let alone interested? The Assembly Hall offered no better facilities for the two classes using the floor of it, separated as they were from each other by a head-high wooden partition; a totally insufficient barrier to dull down the strident tones of Mrs Eileen Edney who was teaching French in the adjacent section, while you tried to initiate your own class into the mysteries of Bismarck's Foreign Policy. Smaller classes (at 'Senior' level) were at the same time situated on the stage behind a dilapidated orange curtain. At

least teaching in the local Orange Hall was a quieter experience, although periods could never begin and end at the scheduled times due to the time taken to saunter up to and down from school. For those in the main building who were taught Latin by W.G. Montgomery (Monty), this was a constant reality as he would enter in a rush some 10 to 15 minutes late and end the class by the same margin after the bell.

In 1960 the school held a Mock Election to coincide with the General Election. All candidates were given the opportunity to deliver their electoral address in the Assembly Hall to the masses and one candidate, fearing that his Nationalist party might struggle to get the attention of the voters, fired a starting-pistol. This shock tactic was effective at the time; however, the number of votes cast for the party was limited.

Form VI A 1960/1

Back left: D. Johnston, W. Harvey and T. Brolly. *Middle left:* M. McConnell, Y. Cushley, E. Campbell, C. Stewart, I. Auld and S. Kirkpatrick. *Front left:* R. Agnew, M. McWhinney, M. Simms, E. Hughes and W. Frazer. *(The Ballyclare High School Archive)*

School prefects 1960/61

Back left: L. Ferron, J. Moffett, B. Peoples, R. Murphy and I. Hunter. *Middle row*: J. Kennedy, J. Smyth, A. Ferguson, E. Laird, B. Logan and F. Newell. *Front left:* D. Harvey, M. Allen, J. Reid, J. Hewitt and W. Horner. *(The Ballyclare High School Archive)*

This photograph from the early 1960s shows three members of staff, Mr J. Stevenson, Mr W.G. Montgomery and Mr L. Francey, on their way to Sports Day. *(The Ballyclare High School Archive)*

The school orchestra in the early 1960s. *(The Ballyclare High School Archive)*

Staff turnover is always volatile, but circumstances meant that by the end of 1962, six members of staff were leaving. Mr James Grainger, the Head of Science who had been responsible for many editions of the school magazine, left in 1962 to become Principal of the new Grammar School in Carrickfergus. Other staff who left were Mrs Eileen Edney, Mrs J.S. Hunter, who achieved a rare double in mothering both a Head Boy and Head Girl at the school, Miss Sheila Crookes, Mr Alan Acheson and the Rev. W.J. Hughes. Of course, in filed new members of staff, one of whom was a Miss S.N. Blair (later Mrs Caldwell) who had a most memorable first encounter with Ballyclare High School. Fresh from London, she arrived for a visit (there had been no interviews) and was met on what was a most inclement day by Mr Russell. After passing the Assembly Hall and along the corridor of the 'aluminium' building, R.E. equipped with his golfing umbrella, said that he would take her on a tour of the rest of the school:

My Chanel suit and shoes were ill-equipped to deal with the large puddle and driving rain, which met us. As I skirted the puddle, Mr Russell in gallant manner (it was the 60s!) waded through it to protect me with the large golfing umbrella. From there, I can truly say that we 'puddle-jumped' our way to the old canteen, a wooden hut named Room 25, where Latin and some French were taught. Thence to the Rope Works and the North End Hut, Mr Russell explaining that he was hopeful about new buildings. Indeed I hoped so too as there was little heating or light and there were holes in the intervening walls through which pupils could communicate during class – if they dared! It was in these huts, the Orange Hall, or in one of the three 'classrooms' or at times four in the Assembly Hall, that my teaching was to be conducted in my early years in Ballyclare High School.

The Games fields were literally that: hay was harvested, sheep grazed and come September, the pitches were marked. There was no P.E. Department for there was no gym, so games were taught by those who had the interest.

By the summer of 1963, the Rope Works had been razed to the ground. That year was also notable as the Duke of Edinburgh Award Scheme commenced. The school magazine for 1964 explained very well the reason for its inception.

In these modern times, the section of the public most maligned, most misunderstood and the most subjected to commercial pressures is the teenage group. Not only do young people have to prepare themselves for careers, but they have to develop in character from the stage of dependent childhood to mature and responsible citizenship. While school life is mostly directed to the acquiring of academic skills, the character-building aspect of education is by no means neglected in education today, but it was felt that even more could be done to help our young people over the difficult transitional years of adolescence.

The Preparatory Department's visit to Stormont in March 1962. The Member of Parliament, Mr N. Minford, can be seen in the middle of the photograph. *(The Ballyclare High School Archive)*

Forms P.V., VI and VII B at Carrickfergus Castle, 1963. *(The Ballyclare High School Archive)*

Ulster Schools' Junior Hockey Cup Winners 1964.
Mrs Pat Moffitt, who taught Modern Languages from 1957 to 1996, played an important role in the success of hockey in the school for many years.
Back row: A. Campbell, M. McChesney, P. McCready, J. Todd, J. McKeown and J. Christie. *Front row:* M. Sherrard, L. Waugh, H. McKeen (Captain), L. Miller and M. Hamill. *(The Ballyclare High School Archive)*

Between 1963 and 1964 significant staff changes took place in the Preparatory Department. Miss M. Adams, a past pupil of the school, was put in charge of the Kindergarten and Miss D. Craig and Miss R. McConnell both left.

Notwithstanding the difficulties concerning the accommodation, the 1960s were great times in many ways for those who both attended and taught in the school. Staff antics have passed down into the school's folklore for their eccentricity, the number of incidents and the fact that so many former members of staff recall that they were just unforgettably funny. One former member of staff, who is definitely not alone, remembers well the mischievous activities of a Biology teacher, Philip Campbell ('PA') (mentioned earlier), appointed at the start of the decade that would bring the Cuban Missile Crisis and unleash the full force of four individuals from Merseyside who helped redefine popular culture:

The school's new front entrance opened in 1965. *(The Ballyclare High School Archive)*

Apparently R.E. Russell thought that he would bring both experience and dignity to the staff. With the former there could be little quibble; as to the latter, R.E.'s judgement was misplaced. Although a man of great culture, 'PA' was an inveterate practical joker: hiding all of the school's blackboard dusters in his Biology lab; inserting on a daily basis into the pocket of T.J. Davidson an empty 1/3 of a pint milk bottle; crawling under the staff dining-table to clip wooden clothes pegs on to the then fashionable stiletto heels of the young female staff. His annual trick occurred during Prize Distribution when all the staff had to be seated on the stage of the Old Assembly Hall, ladies in the front rows. Philip Campbell would manage to tie the tails of their gowns to their chairs and, when the National Anthem was played to end the proceedings, they were forced to arise and stand in a most undignified fashion.

Mr Russell had delayed retirement in order to be at the helm when the new buildings were opened at last. Indeed, such was the state of his health that he missed the Prize Distribution in 1965. When the buildings were opened in the same year, they brought a new Gymnasium and a plethora of new rooms for Geography, Chemistry, Biology and Physics. Much to the relief of those responsible for Physical Education, new changing-rooms were also included. By 1965 the school's cricket teams at last had a satisfactory field to play on.

The changes during Mr Russell's 27 years as Principal were enormous. When he joined the school in 1939, there were 150 pupils taught by 8 staff. When he left in 1966, this had grown to 730 and a staff of 40.

This aerial photograph taken in 1971 shows the various locations of what became Ballyclare High School and its well-known features. *(Ballymena Times and Observer, December 16th 1971)*

1 The location of Miss Aikin's first school building in Ballyclare, at the top of the Square, after her move from Doagh in 1904.

2 The school's first site on the Rashee Road from 1916.

3 Mr Fowweather's 'new school building' opened in 1930.

4 The extension opened by the Duchess of Abercorn in 1938.

5 Part of the major extension of Mr Russell's era opened in 1965.

6 The location of what used to be the North End Hut.

7 The location of what became known as the Rope Works or the Morgue.

8 The location of what used to be the cleansing station.

J.D. Williams – appointed Principal in 1966.
(The Ballyclare High School Archive)

H.A. Mudd – Acting Principal.
(The Ballyclare High School Archive)

Upon Mr Russell's retirement, the new Principal was Mr J.D. Williams. He had joined the school in 1946 and had gone on to become Head of History. This pattern would be repeated in later years when another Head of History, Robert FitzPatrick, became Principal in 1990. Mr Williams was a native of Kerry and a graduate of Trinity College, Dublin, where he read History and Political Science. It was in Ballyclare High School that Mr Williams met his future wife, who was a teacher of German. Incidentally, in Mr Williams' first year there was further sporting success for the school: W. Morrison won a medal in the All Ireland Cross-Country Championships.

Mr Williams' Headship was relatively short, lasting from 1966 to 1971, when he died on New Year's Day, after a brief illness, at the age of 51. He believed passionately that Ballyclare High School needed its own proper library. At the dedication of the new library, constructed as part of the school's huge extension in the mid-1980s, the Rev. H.R. Allen, minister of Ballyclare Presbyterian Church, reminded those present of Mr Williams'

views and noted that it was most fitting for the library to be called the "J.D. Williams Memorial Library". Staff who served under Mr Williams' Headship remember how he used regularly to articulate his concerns about the inadequate library provision at staff meetings. During Mr Williams' short tenure he extended the House System in two ways. Firstly, Russell was added and secondly the House System was from then to include not only athletic, but also academic achievements. He also introduced the Honours Blazers which are still a source of considerable pride for those who have attained them.

On the death of Mr Williams, the school's acting Principal was Mr H.A. Mudd, until the arrival of Mr Millar in 1971. Mr Mudd had been appointed Vice-Principal in 1968, succeeding T.J. Davidson. He graduated from the University College of North Wales, Bangor, and had served in the Royal Welsh Fusiliers during the Second World War. He was appointed to teach English and History in 1946 and became Head of English the following year.

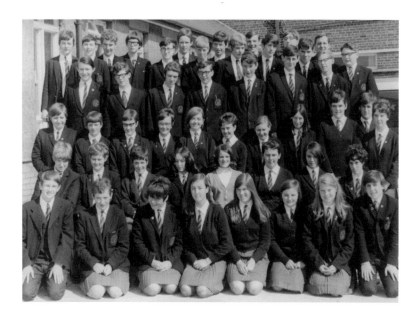

A year group photograph of Lower Sixth in 1968.
Front row (left to right kneeling): E. Mitchell, E. White, M. McDowell, R. McCullough, A. Redding, R. Stevenson, F. Black and G. McKinley.
Sitting (left to right): P. Stirling, B. Barr, S. Jones, J. Withers, Miss Olive McKenzie, H. Siberry, L. Moffett and D. Close. *Standing (girls left to right):* I. Burns, M. Sherrard, B. Reid, M. Stewart, S. Andrew, S. Beggs, A. Wilson, B. Moore, M. McAllister, A. Mayne and to rear at right R. Meighan.
Standing (boys left to right): B. Crotty, T. Curran, J. Kyle, B. Neill, N. Todd, A. McCracken, W. Weatherup and R. McMillen. *Standing (left to right):* F. Henderson, B. Millar, H. Laughlin, C. Bennett, N. McCracken, D. Bryson, T. Moreland, P. Nesbitt, M. Greer, T. Elliott, R. Mairs, J. Stewart, ?, R. White. In the year of the school's centenary, two former pupils in this photograph, Dr Robert McMillen and Miss Maureen Stewart are Chairman of the Board of Governors and Vice-Principal respectively. *(The Ballyclare High School Archive)*

Chapter 3

Glorious Ravenhill to "We need to be careful that we don't turn this into a normal school"

The school's new Principal was appointed in July 1971. A former pupil of Banbridge Academy, Cecil Millar was a Queen's University graduate. He was a Vice-Principal at Lurgan College when he was appointed to Ballyclare High. Mr Millar remembers his feelings of anticipation at the challenge of assuming the position and the innovations that were one of the hallmarks of his first year as Principal.

I am sure every Headteacher on taking up position has dreams for their school, and, some thirty years ago, I was no exception. I wanted my school to be good academically, but I knew that to achieve this was only part of any young person's education for life. The activities of the school outside the classroom would also play an important part in the change from child to adult.

That first year saw the start of the Prefects' Christmas Dinners, the Prefects' Formal Dances, the first Parent-Staff meeting and the first Careers Advice meeting for Forms III and V. A change from a minimum seven subjects to a minimum eight subjects for each pupil taking G.C.E. was introduced, and the number of fee-paying pupils entering the school was cut by 75%. The latter decisions caused some concern amongst staff, but were vindicated when the next year saw the qualified pupil intake rise from 100 to 160, and

during the next nineteen years, the total enrolment always increased. This was quite an achievement, and certainly the school buildings were not the attraction, as the North Eastern Board's only solution was to place another mobile on an already crowded site. It is to the great credit of the staff and pupils that these drawbacks did not diminish their enthusiasm or academic results.

In the early years of Mr Millar's tenure it was obvious that the idea mooted during the late 1960s, that the school could become a Sixth Form college, would not come to fruition.

Saturday, March 17th 1973, was indeed a red-letter day in the school's history. At Ravenhill, the 1st XV pulled off an impressive 13-8 win against Royal Belfast Academical Institution to bring the Schools' Cup to Ballyclare for the first and, as yet, only time. The sense of anticipation had been palpable. The Director of Education of the Antrim County Education Committee, Dr R.J. Dickson, had written to the Principal two days before the Final, noting that "this is the first time that a County grammar school in Antrim has reached the Final and we could have no better or worthy representatives than Ballyclare High School".

Ravenhill was packed for the match, with many hundreds pouring in from Ballyclare and surrounding areas. After the win,

G.C.G. Millar – appointed Principal in 1971.
(The Ballyclare High School Archive)

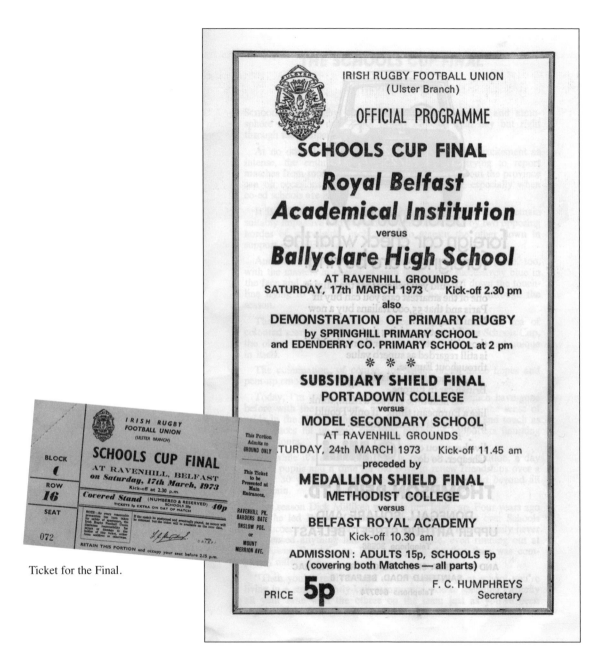

IRISH RUGBY FOOTBALL UNION
(Ulster Branch)

OFFICIAL PROGRAMME

SCHOOLS CUP FINAL

Royal Belfast
Academical Institution

versus

Ballyclare High School

AT RAVENHILL GROUNDS
SATURDAY, 17th MARCH 1973   Kick-off 2.30 pm

also

DEMONSTRATION OF PRIMARY RUGBY
by SPRINGHILL PRIMARY SCHOOL
and EDENDERRY CO. PRIMARY SCHOOL at 2 pm

* * *

SUBSIDIARY SHIELD FINAL

PORTADOWN COLLEGE

versus

MODEL SECONDARY SCHOOL

AT RAVENHILL GROUNDS
SATURDAY, 24th MARCH 1973   Kick-off 11.45 am

preceded by

MEDALLION SHIELD FINAL

METHODIST COLLEGE

versus

BELFAST ROYAL ACADEMY

Kick-off 10.30 am

ADMISSION : ADULTS 15p, SCHOOLS 5p
(covering both Matches — all parts)

PRICE **5p**

F. C. HUMPHREYS
Secretary

IRISH RUGBY
FOOTBALL UNION
(ULSTER BRANCH)

SCHOOLS CUP FINAL

AT RAVENHILL, BELFAST
on Saturday, 17th March, 1973
Kick-off at 2.30 p.m.

BLOCK 1
ROW 16
SEAT 072

Covered Stand (NUMBERED & RESERVED)
SCHOOLS 25p   40p
TICKETS 5p EXTRA ON DAY OF MATCH

This Portion
Admits to
GROUND ONLY

This Ticket
to be
Presented at
Main
Entrances,
RAVENHILL PK.
BARDENS GATE
ONSLOW PDE.
or
MOUNT
MERRION AVE.

RETAIN THIS PORTION and occupy your seat before 2.15 p.m.

Ticket for the Final.

plaudits flowed in from not just the surrounding area, but from all over Northern Ireland and further afield. Primary schools, traders, churches, parents, past pupils, and of course the local Council all sent in warm letters of congratulation. Mr T. McBride, the Chairman of Newtownabbey Urban District Council, stated:

My fellow Councillors and I were delighted to hear of the school's success in the Schools' Cup. This is an outstanding achievement which reflects great credit on everyone concerned. May I, on behalf of the members of this Council, and on my own behalf, offer you our heartiest congratulations.

Frank Gault, a member of the victorious team who now teaches Chemistry in the school, in addition to coaching the 1st XV, remembers the match and the reception the team got when they presented the Cup to the school in Assembly the following Monday.

We were told before the Final to enjoy the day and the experience, as it would all pass in the blink of an eye. The naivety of youth scoffed at such nonsense, but it was good advice, wasted on deaf ears. My memories of the day are like snapshots, frozen moments of time.

We arrived about an hour before the scheduled kick-off (I don't even remember the actual time) and installed ourselves in the 'away' changing-room. We quickly went out to 'inspect the pitch' and take in the atmosphere. The spectators were starting to assemble and I can recall chants and cheers coming from the terracing and promenade areas. Then the match started. It was frenetic and intense. We had no doubts we were going to win. Inst. made a ferocious start. We defended and defended. It seemed relentless. Willie John Hutchinson raced back to cover a kick through and save a score. Gradually we began to settle and make some inroads into the Inst. defence. From a ruck, Inst. were penalised, Nigel Simpson kicked the penalty and suddenly we were in the lead.

1st XV 1972-73 Winners of the Ulster Schools' Challenge Cup
Back row standing: Mr D. Armstrong, S.A. Houston, J. Millar, L.N. Smith, I.R. McIlwaine, Mr G.C.G. Millar, H.C. Coy, A.S. Siberry, J. Gault and
Mr W.G. Montgomery. *Seated:* W.J. Hutchinson, J.B. Whincup, N.J. Simpson, W.A. Gleghorne (Captain), R.W. Gilmer (Vice-Captain), F. Gault and J.F. McCreary.
Seated at front: S.O. Gilmer and D.I. McKeown. *(The Ballyclare High School Archive)*

Mr R. McKay, Head of Music. *(The Ballyclare High School Archive)*

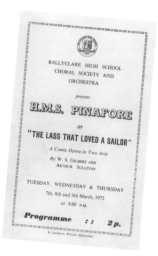

Cover of the programme for the first school opera.

A second penalty followed and then as I rose from a ruck I could see Leslie Smith make a searing break through the Inst. defence to score a try. Almost half-time and we were 10 – 0 in front (4 points for a try in those olden days). The course of the match changed in a 10 minute period.

Into the second half and the Inst. onslaught continued. It was our defence against their attack, but eventually our defence cracked and Inst. scored two quick tries. The score stood at 10 – 8, with one conversion missed and another to come. As I stood under the posts waiting for the second conversion, I turned to James McCreary beside me and said, "If he kicks this, we're in trouble". The conversion was missed and all doubt left me.

Nigel Simpson kicked a third penalty to make the score 13 – 8. Although Inst. resumed their onslaught on our try-line, we held firm. With the last move of the match, Colin Patterson, their scrum-half and later a British Lion, was bundled into touch when he seemed certain to score. The final whistle sounded and we were engulfed by the charging supporters as they invaded the pitch.

The rest of the weekend passed in a blur. We toured Ballyclare on the back of a milk float (I still cringe at the thought of it), went to the 'Pig n' Chicken' (now the Templeton) for a reception and were mentioned in church sermons the next morning.

On the Monday we gathered, seated on the stage in the gym, curtains closed. The curtains opened to a wall of sound; people hanging off the wall-bars, cleaning staff, kitchen staff, teaching staff and fellow pupils, all a heaving, shouting mass. It was overwhelming and finally began to bring home the magnitude of the achievement.

It is only from the distance given by time that the full experience can be appreciated; the impact on the school community and the local community evaluated. For many years after and even today people remember the occasion and ask, "Were you one of the Gault twins who played in the Cup Final?" I still find it surprising that people remember the event and humbling to be associated with such a momentous happening in the history of the school.

Still, if he had kicked that second conversion, we might have been in trouble.

At a time when the reputation of sportsmen and women has never been under greater scrutiny, it is noteworthy that over thirty years ago so many people wrote to the school and paid tribute to the display of such sportsmanship. One former pupil wrote in 1973: "At a time when tolerance in sport and forbearance in Northern Ireland are at a low ebb, it was refreshing to see the sportsmanship adopted by all the players". One Belfast outfitters who provided the school's uniform was particularly pleased to see the Cup going to a 'country school'! Needless to say, the historic first for the school featured prominently in the Principal's speech at Prize Night on November 9th 1973. Mr Millar noted: "For me, in only my second year with you, it was one of the greatest moments of my life". He also thanked the Council for presenting each member of the team with a memorial plaque, as well as for giving a plaque to the school containing the names of the winning team.

The school year 1971 had heralded the beginnings of the first of the now well-known and much loved school operas. Messrs Roy McKay and Ivor Stinson put on the first performance of *H.M.S. Pinafore* at the request of the new Principal. Mr Millar favoured light opera because there had been a concern that some potential school plays might attract unwarranted attention. An early difficulty was the hesitation of some, and outright reluctance of other, senior boys to participate in what some viewed was a rather 'sissy' exercise. However, Mr Millar provided suitable 'encouragement' and casting did not prove to be an insurmountable problem after all. Accompaniment was provided by the school orchestra of 15, directed by Roy McKay who also played the piano. In the first year of performance, 1972, the costumes were made by Miss Irene Green, herself a viola player, and the set was designed by Mr Jim Rafferty.

Such was the success of the first season, with three full houses, it was decided that the school should extend the opera season to a full week, with the next performance scheduled for February 1973.

As is typical of show business, there has never been any shortage of drama – both on and off stage. Robert FitzPatrick, a keen stalwart of the orchestra for many years, recalled:

I was there on the night Ivor Stinson got stuck in his revolving portrait in Ruddigore, and on the nights when in Iolanthe the whine of the fork-lift truck (which had been brought in at no little expense or trouble to raise Iolanthe through the trap/pond onto the stage) drowned out her finely-modulated tones. Or am I forgetting that she may have been choking in the clouds of carbon dioxide, which simulated the marshy mists?

Mr FitzPatrick's family had been well represented in the orchestra, with his son Craig playing trombone, and daughter Deborah playing violin, in addition to his own contribution on the double bass. Mr John Dallas, who took over the baton in 1976, recalled some drama surrounding the production of *The Pirates of Penzance* and *The Gondoliers*:

The 1990 production of The Pirates of Penzance included one very scary moment. As the end of Act 1 approached one night, I was walking down the corridor outside the theatre (sorry P.E. staff…gym) where I found the crumpled form of Sharon Reynolds who was playing Ruth that year. She had fainted and was due to go on stage before the end of the Act. A quick message was smuggled to Roy McKay who was able to cut that part and luckily she was able to go on for the rest of the week.
  Of the two productions of The Gondoliers performed here, my main memory is the upending of the Gondola due to a rather large Duke of Plaza Toro stepping on (or off) at the wrong time. Ah well, I'm sure real Gondolas can sink too!

Seared into Maestro Dallas' memory is the incident of the dove in *La Belle Hélène*, which flew in every night, flapping wings and all. The trouble was that one night it decided to do the backstroke and came in upside down!

Mr I. Stinson photographed from *Ruddigore* in 1976. Ivor Stinson joined the school in 1950, teaching Junior Science and Mathematics. He was the Musical Director of seven Gilbert and Sullivan operettas. *(The Ballyclare High School Archive)*

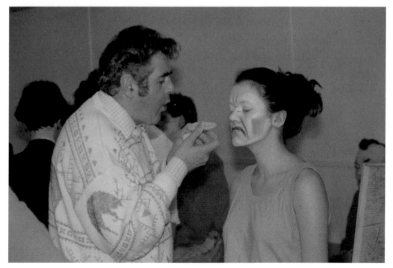

Preparing for the Gala Performance of *The Mikado* in 1989: Mr J.R. Dallas and A. Moore. *(The Ballyclare High School Archive)*

The U16 Badminton Team from 1980 that was the first team to win an Irish Schools title. *Back left:* C. Porter and I. Richardson *(Coach). Front left:* M. Turkington, S. Thompson and S. Stewart. *(The Ballyclare High School Archive)*

Professor J.W. Dundee *(far right),* a distinguished former pupil of the school, was the guest at the school's Prize Distribution in 1982. Also pictured are Mr Millar, Mrs Dundee, and Mr S. Cameron (Chairman of the Board of Governors). *(The Ballyclare High School Archive)*

Of course, there are countless anecdotes regarding Music in the school. For instance, at Assembly one morning, a senior member of staff who was unacquainted with the pronunciation of a particular musical instrument read out the following announcement.

Any pupil who would be interested in acquiring a double bass see Mr McKay in the music-room before the end of break.

To the amusement of the assembled masses, the word 'bass' was pronounced as in the well-known alcoholic brand name.

Roy McKay, a former Head of Music, recalled that it wasn't just at the school opera or Assembly that events could take a particular turn:

During the performance of a piece at one of the annual Orchestral Concerts a young second violinist who had over-indulged in potato crisps and chocolate, deposited the contents of her stomach on the floor in front of the conductor. Not wanting to stop the performance in full flight, the conductor continued undaunted. However, the arrival of this unwanted 'material' alerted the double-bass player (Mr FitzPatrick) to take action before the audience was overcome by the malodorous substance. He hastily went out and returned with a bucket of water well treated with Jeyes Fluid, plus a mop, and proceeded to wipe the floor to the accompaniment of Handel's 'Music for the Royal Fireworks'.

June 1980 brought the retirement of the Senior Mistress, Miss J. M. Hall, and a former Acting Principal and Vice-Principal, Mr H.A. Mudd. The first year of the new decade also brought football to the school in an organised manner. Pupils had played the game for many years, usually at lunchtime, but this was unofficial and the school did not actively enter teams in competitions. However, in the 1950s and 1960s, pupils put themselves in a grammar schools' league that was organised by Cliftonville Football Club. These teams were not permitted to use the name of the school as

Winners of the Esso Schools' Cup 1991. Mr T. Stewart who started organised football in the school is pictured with Mr FitzPatrick, and the winning side that consisted of: B. Todd, S. Collier, G. Lutton, G. Smith, S. Arthur, D. McLean, A. McKeown, G. McKeen, N. Snoddy, J. Armstrong, A. Huxley, D. Brocklehurst and P. Thompson (Captain – holding the trophy).
(T. Stewart Collection)

The victorious Stockpiler Team from 1978. *From left to right:* T. Maze, R. Simpson, H. Stevenson, D. Wylie, M. Douglas and O. Rea. *(The Ballyclare High School Archive)*

R.E. had sanctioned only rugby and cross-country as official male sports. As soccer became more settled in the timetable, numerous teams were having increasing success, not least in the East Antrim Cup. In 1991 Ballyclare High reached the top of competitive school football when a very talented team played the Boys' Model in the Final at Chimney Corner's ground. Ballyclare won 2-1.

Ironically, before pupils got a chance to play properly-organised competitive football the High School had a key role in developing the talents of a future Northern Ireland captain. Tommy Wright attended from 1973 to 1978 and, after playing for Linfield, left for a career in the English League. With spells at Newcastle United and Manchester City, amongst others, he was voted Northern Ireland Player of the Year in 1993 and 1997, in addition to winning 31 full international caps. Tommy's athleticism in school was renowned, as he had excelled at cross-country and athletics. Indeed, in the 1977/78 season, he became the All-Ireland Cross-Country Champion.

In today's climate, when the curriculum is geared increasingly towards employability and key skills, it is interesting to note that pupils from Ballyclare have a long tradition of excelling in competitions and activities where they have an opportunity to exercise their business acumen. In April 1978 a team of 'tycoons in the making' travelled to London, led by Mr Millar and the teacher responsible, Wilbert Hollinger. The six boys had won the Stockpiler competition that had been sponsored by Williams & Glyn's Bank and organised by the British Junior Chamber of Commerce. The thrust of the competition was to manage an imaginary portfolio worth £20,000 on the London stock market and to try to increase the value of the holdings by buying and selling shares. The Ballyclarians beat nearly 2,000 other teams to claim first prize. Their stock portfolio had soared by an amazing 61% over 5 months at a time when the *Financial Times* Ordinary Share Index fell by 10.2%. Many fund managers in the City could only look on with envy at this astonishingly impressive performance. The team, who were all aged 17, was led by Trevor Maze. They, with Mr Millar and Mr Hollinger, were lavished with transport in Rolls Royces, dinner with the Bank's Board of Directors and a presentation of the Stockpiler trophy in the Bakers' Hall.

The school went on to have other success in nurturing young business talent. For example, a four-man team came second in a competition run by Coopers & Lybrand in 1988/89 which again gave students an imaginary unit trust portfolio valued at £20,000. They had to buy and sell shares to increase the value of the trust.

Over the years many of Ballyclare High's staff and pupils have met various members of the Royal family in recognition of their achievements. One example took place in 1979. In June of that year the Rev. Jack Moore of North Belfast Mission had come to talk to a Scripture Union meeting in the school. It was suggested that some pupils might volunteer to help redecorate a holiday home for underprivileged senior citizens and young people. Funding was provided by the Prince's Trust and seven girls from the school spent a sizeable chunk of the summer developing some key skills. In relation to his work with Scripture Union, and this project specifically, Biology teacher Brian Griffith went to Buckingham Palace to meet Prince Charles. After this encounter, Mr Griffith commented that the Prince had been "well briefed and asked numerous questions on the pupils' efforts". Mr Griffith also earned himself a lunch in the delightful surroundings of Fortnum and Mason.

Reputation and image are vital for all institutions, no matter their field of interest, and therefore most schools would be very wary of having a story featuring them splashed all over the front page of a province-wide newspaper. On Thursday, December 14th 1978, a large bold headline read: "Revolt threat at school of shame".

Sydney Cameron, the chairman of the Management Committee, expressed concern in late 1978 and early 1979 that the High School was being held to ransom as the Government was determined to impose a comprehensive system of education. The North-Eastern Education and Library Board invited the school to put forward its views. Mr Cameron noted: "I have no doubt that the majority, if not all the Committee members, will insist that Ballyclare High retains its role as a grammar school to meet the need in the area". He went on to say that talking about waiting for a comprehensive system was "only confusing the main issue: the replacement of the present primitive conditions to bring the school buildings into the modern age. Whatever the future of the school is to be – if it must be comprehensive – new permanent buildings will have to be provided". Only a few months earlier, the 60 members of the teaching staff issued a statement that they would not "continue to tolerate the sub-standard conditions". Concerned parents had written to their local Member of Parliament to articulate their outrage at the conditions in the school. Mr James Molyneaux M.P., who had seen service in 1939-45, likened the school to a war camp

when he visited in January 1979. He was shocked that approximately 70% of the school's teaching rooms were comprised of huts in the school playground. He was surprised that the morale of the staff remained so high. After being shown around the school by Mr Millar, Mr Molyneaux noted that the school "needed more than just a facelift" and commented that key staff had to work in "cubbyholes". One parent with three children at the school wrote in the *News Letter*, to Dr Dickson, the Chief Officer of the North Eastern Education and Library Board:

Senior Boys' Athletics Team 1983. Winners of the Irish Schools' Athletics Association College of Science Cup (large cup). The smaller cup for the Relay Team is on the left of the picture and the silver baton for being the Irish Schools' Champions is on the right. *From left:* M. Clyde, M. Forsythe, R. Robinson (Captain), P. Snoddy and M. McKinstry. *(The Ballyclare High School Archive)*

Ballyclare High School was intended to give educational facilities to approximately 500 pupils. It now caters for over 1,000 pupils and a very large percentage of these pupils are being taught in temporary buildings. The accommodation available for the pupils is as follows:

11 regulation size classrooms – all specialist rooms; 6 (temporary) aluminium classrooms; 24 mobile units; 1 gymnasium; 1 assembly hall.

Based on the above information only 24% of pupils are accommodated in permanent classrooms. This is a disgraceful state of affairs and must be remedied immediately. The area that contains the mobile huts is particularly bad, especially at this time of the year. The walkways between the huts are not covered and whenever it rains, which is frequently, the underfoot and overhead conditions are intolerable. Add to this the fact that many pupils have to carry their raincoats around the school, because of inadequate cloakroom facilities, and you can imagine how uncomfortable teachers and pupils are by the end of the day.

Another parent signed her letter 'Disgusted and Sickened' after writing:

As a parent of two girls presently attending, I am horrified to know that toilets require to be used as changing accommodation with clothes left lying on the floor, that moving from mobile to mobile in all sorts of weather with no hope of drying out for the rest of the day is commonplace and that such modern amenities as a library, language laboratory, sick room, lecture theatre, sports pavilion, or music practice rooms are non-existent.

Pupils too weighed in, and wrote to the Press articulating their feelings. Some in Year 11 complained about the appalling lack of changing facilities for sporting teams. Their frustration and embarrassment are all too evident in this brief extract of yet another published letter in the provincial Press:

The school's mobiles in 1984. In a written answer to a parliamentary question asked by the Rev. Ian Paisley M.P. the year before, the Minister responsible for Education, Mr Nicholas Scott M.P., replied that 26 temporary classrooms had been in use for periods ranging from 6 to 19 years. *(The Ballyclare High School Archive)*

With the lack of facilities visiting teams have to change before they arrive or in the Assembly Hall or in a classroom. This is especially embarrassing for the captains, as they have to show the visitors where to change and continually hear complaints from team members of the visiting teams. We would like to draw your attention to the fact that when it is impossible to go outside there is nowhere for all the pupils to do games inside. Due to this lack of sports halls many pupils miss necessary sports practice.

Such was the mounting storm over the lack of facilities that the editorial in the *News Letter* even singled out the school. On January 25th 1979 the 'Morning View' stated:

For many months the bad accommodation at the school has been given a lot of publicity with commentators searching for tough enough adjectives. The only other complex to receive such space in newspapers and time on TV and radio in the Province has been the Maze prison, where the occupants and not the accommodation – as at Ballyclare High School – are the problem.

The school's problems with inadequate accommodation have been well documented and the photograph from 1984 shows the assembled multitude of mobile classrooms. Eventually, after a campaign lasting over a decade, work on new buildings commenced and, by 1986, the move into three phases of the new premises had begun. By this stage, enrolment was in excess of 1,000 pupils and on Wednesday, May 6th 1987, the Duchess of Abercorn performed the official opening.

The new school buildings were handed over to the school by the contractor, Mr C. Blackbourne. This was a proud moment for Mr Blackbourne whose son had been murdered by the IRA while serving in the Royal Ulster Constabulary. Many who attended the opening ceremony remarked that the most moving part of the proceedings was when a bell was dedicated to the memory of Karl Blackbourne. Karl was 19 years old when he was killed in a terrorist attack on July 26th 1986. The Rev. Clyde Irvine, Head of

The Old Ballyclarians' Golden Jubilee Dinner in 1985. *From left:* Mr and Mrs G.C.G. Millar, Mr and Mrs Fowweather, the Mayor and Mayoress (Cllr and Mrs L. Caul), Mr N. Cinnamon (President, O.B.A.) and Mrs Cinnamon and Mr D. Moore (Chairman, O.B.A.) and Mrs Moore. *(R. McMillen Collection)*

Dr R.M. McMillen, who proposed the toast to the Association, with Mrs McMillen, C. FitzPatrick (Head Boy) and S. Parke (Head Girl). *(R. McMillen Collection)*

Building of the Sports Hall. (*G.C.G. Millar Collection*)

The Duchess of Abercorn performs the official opening of the new buildings.
(*The Ballyclare High School Archive*)

An aerial view, from the west, of the school in 1987. (*The Ballyclare High School Archive*)

Religious Education, noted that Karl "spent 14 years of his life in this school, attending class, engaging in sport and enjoying the company of friends. An important part of his life was spent at school and from Primary One to Upper Sixth he always gave of his best". The new buildings cost nearly £4 million and in a twist of history it was an earlier Duchess of Abercorn who had opened a school extension in 1938 that cost the princely sum of £8,000. It is more than Chancellors of the Exchequer who feel the chilly winds of inflation!

Mrs Blackbourne unveils a bell erected at the back of the Sports Hall in honour of her late son Karl. *(The Ballyclare High School Archive)*

The design of the new buildings meant that, for the first time, there was to be one large staffroom. Prior to this, the female staffroom was located in what is now the Principal's office and the male staffroom was a room off the same landing that is now used by the Vice-Principals. The Principal's office used to be centred in the General Office, overlooking what is now the Millennium Garden. The new buildings took the school into an age of relative affluence. The facilities included a new kitchen and dining area, an arts and languages section, a new main teaching block with 15 classrooms, a student common room, a library and Biology block, a sports hall with nine changing-rooms and purpose-built tennis courts.

In his speech at the official opening of the new buildings, Mr Millar expressed his hopes for the future:

We can surely say that our buildings are 'a thing of beauty', whether they will be a 'joy forever' remains to be seen, but with them and the dedication of staff and pupils, the future of the school could not be brighter. Perhaps we shall get back to enjoying our schooldays once again.

The mid to late 1980s brought a raft of educational changes, such as the ending of corporal punishment and the introduction of GCSEs, and these were never far from the mind of Mr Millar. In his Prize Day address in 1989, he described them as "probably the biggest shake-up in the educational world" in four decades. A year earlier the Board of Governors had named the Sports Hall the Montgomery Hall after W.G. Montgomery, or Monty, who had been such a stalwart of school sport, in addition to being Head of Classics. Changes in staff were also particularly significant during the latter half of the 1980s. In 1986 Dr Roderick Acheson joined

Mr W.G. Montgomery at the opening of the new Sports Hall named in his honour, with Mr Millar and former pupil Mark Forsythe who represented Great Britain in the 1988 Olympic Games. *(The Ballyclare High School Archive)*

The Medallion Shield Winners 1990. *Back left:* Mr G.C.G. Millar, R. Glenn, T. Ervine, J. Armstrong, M. Crothers, D. Dunlop, Mr R. Hassard, J. Luke, S. Crawford, D. Bell, P. Kerr, J. Lowe and Mr T.S. Young (Head of Physical Education). *Front left:* N. Crothers, T. Brown, J. Anderson, D. Bingham, J. Montgomery, S. Arthur (Captain), A. McIlwaine, G. Smith, D. McIlroy, B. Kerr and G. Alexander. *(The Ballyclare High School Archive)*

the Senior Staff and in 1989 two Vice-Principals were appointed. Miss Maureen Stewart and Mr Wilbert Hollinger were two former pupils of the school. Mrs Nan Caldwell, Mr Ronnie Hassard and Mrs Joan Allen also joined the Senior Staff.

During the 1980s the school held many of its highly successful Reunion Dinners, organised by Mrs Mary Williams and Mrs Nan Caldwell. At such occasions many friendships were renewed and numerous speakers told many amusing anecdotes about the conditions at the school during the 1940s and 1950s.

The use of computers has brought Ballyclare High many accolades. In 1987, pupils won five out of a possible eight prizes at the 'Memory Computer Competition', organised by Memory Computer plc. The awards ceremony, at the Gresham Hotel in Dublin, was yet another occasion for the school to be publicly recognised as a leader in the use of ICT in teaching and learning. Tony Campbell took first prize of £150 in the junior individual section with his computerised telescope, which also won an award

in a competition run by Aer Lingus. The Irish Minister of Education, Mrs Mary O'Rourke, presented the awards. Richard Wallace, teacher-in-charge, remarked at the time that Mrs O'Rourke was "very interested in our work and sees the North of Ireland as very much leading the way": prophetic words when one considers the success the school would have in the new millennium.

Rugby success came again in 1990 when Ballyclare High won the Medallion Shield. Echoing the Schools' Cup victory in 1973, the Final was held at Ravenhill and the Medallion XV defeated Coleraine Academical Institution 8-4. This had been the school's first appearance in the Final.

The Under-14s won a seven-a-side tournament held at Ballymena Academy in the same year. Success on the rugby field had ushered in the Millar era and was now seeing it out as the Principal retired the same year. Hockey also had its share of success, when the U14As were runners-up in the Junior Cup.

The Staff 1989

Back row left: R. Acheson, W. Hollinger, P. Leckey, J. Rafferty, J. Whincup, F. Gault, T. Stewart, R. Hassard, T. Coleman, R. Shields, J. Dallas, B. Griffith, T. Martin and I. Gracey. *Fourth row left:* T. Thomlinson, C. Irvine, M. Barr, R. Hanna, S. Thompson, J. Dougan, T. Young, R. Wallace, N. Browne, T. Mullan, L. Reid and R. McKay.
Third row left: S. Bell, E. Mayne, M. McKeown, C. Branagh, J. Caves, Y. Magee, M. Mackay, J. Adamson, N. Caldwell, J. Scott, R. Carlisle, P. Moffitt and B. Dyer.
Second row left: A. Heaney, G. Woodside, J. Allen, S. Watson, E. Wilson, J. Chesney, S. Grant, O. Lamont, N. Alexander, S. Duke, J. Ramsay, C. Nicholl and F. Moore.
Front row left: J. Cree, V. Lorrimer, M. Stewart, J. Wilson, A. Weatherup, R. Thornbury, M. Williams, G.C.G. Millar (Principal), L. Francey, S. Bell, T. McClintock,
C. Millar, H. Young and I. McKenna. *Not present:* D. Kernohan, A. Francey and V. Johnston. *(The Ballyclare High School Archive)*

R.J. FitzPatrick – appointed Principal in 1990. *(The Ballyclare High School Archive)*

Robert FitzPatrick, who had huge experience of the school, as teacher of History, Head of History and Vice-Principal, succeeded Mr Millar as Principal. He had left the school in 1984 to join the Inspectorate before returning in 1990. In 1991, Mr Richard Wallace was appointed Vice-Principal and Mr Trevor Martin and Mr John Dougan, both former pupils, were promoted to the Senior Staff. The school year 1991/92 brought outstanding success in athletics. In all, seven pupils were selected for the Ulster Schools' Athletics team. Four pupils, Jonathan Anderson, Nigel Carlisle, Eoin McKinney and Heather Wright, represented Ireland. Eoin became the British champion at 400m and Jonathan became the European champion at 200m. Also that year, the 1st XV reached the quarter-finals of the Schools' Cup and the Medallion won the

Pupil A. Robson, third from left, with Dr Helen Sharman the first British woman in space at a Physics conference, Queen's University, Belfast, June 1993. *(The Ballyclare High School Archive)*

Plate by beating the Royal School, Dungannon. In 1991 the school's long involvement with School Aid Romania began. Ballyclare High has forged close links with Methodist College, Belfast, and St. Patrick's College, Maghera, in this cross-community venture that brings Sixth Form pupils together to help the people of Romania. Since its inception thousands of pounds have been raised and four Montgomery Transport containers have been filled on two different occasions. In addition, parents of pupils who have gone out with the trips have adopted three girls.

In 1992 the Old Ballyclarians' Association met for a very special occasion. This was the official opening of the O.B.A. pavilion in its grounds on the Doagh Road. The aim was to have a focal point for the O.B.A. and to provide support for sport, especially for the Rugby Club that managed the building. Very appropriately, the guest for the official opening was none other than Arthur Fowweather who had played such a seminal role in the school's first half-century.

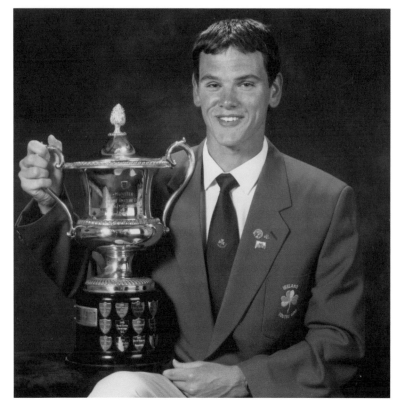

Johnny Foster, Irish International Golfer 1998-2003, pictured with the Munster Youth Trophy won in 1997. In 1997 Johnny was the runner-up in the Senior Ulster Boys' Championship and in 1997 won both the Ulster and Munster Youth Titles. *(The Ballyclare High School Archive)*

In 1993 the school had great success in athletics as Ballyclare High came top out of 140 schools competing in the Ulster Championships. The victorious athletes won the Overall Girls and Boys Cups. *Back left:* Members of staff, Mr J. Whincup, Mr J. Dougan, Mrs J. Adamson, Mr J. Rafferty and Mr T. Young. *Second row from back, to second row from front.* G. Caughey, L. Baker, L. Montgomery, L. McGookin, K. Carson, J. Lynas, A. Dunlop, L. Hurst, J. Sloan, G. Robinson, R. McKinney, G. McMeekin, A. Sweeney, G. Ervine, N. Lendrum, R. Currie, H. Wright, J. Lowe, J. Boyd, R. Treacy, E. McKinney, G. McKee, D. Lendrum, N. Carlisle, J. Steven, M. Brown and D. Lowe. *Front left:* E. McKinney, J. Woodside, P. Lynas, B. Kerr, J. Anderson, F. Lynas, R. Ardill and P. Calvert. *(The Ballyclare High School Archive)*

Ballyclare High has taken pride in its European connections for many years, and further evidence of this was when the school sent a delegation headed by Mr and Mrs FitzPatrick to Dorsten, Germany, for the 350th anniversary celebrations of the Gymnasium Petrinum in 1992. Some of the pupils who went for the week noted: "It was an ideal opportunity for us to forge lasting friendships with people from a foreign culture". The link with Dorsten had been established in 1990. In 1992 the school was the only Northern Ireland school to win one of the 6 European Curriculum Awards that had been created to mark the United Kingdom's Presidency of the European Community. In addition to the German link with Dorsten, from 1995 the school has been twinned with Lycée Camille Sée in Colmar, Alsace. This has proved to be another very successful link, particularly for A Level French students who have the chance to stay with a French family for a week, visit the European Parliament in Strasbourg and then reciprocate their stay by hosting French pupils the following year in Ballyclare. Many an international friendship has begun in this way.

In November 1996, 22 senior students, accompanied by Mrs L. Doherty, Mrs G. Woodside and Mr T. Stewart, visited the Gymnasium Petrinum in Dorsten. This photograph was taken outside the town hall where they had been welcomed by the mayor, Dr Zahn. *(The Ballyclare High School Archive)*

Mr Jean-Pierre Radigue and Mr R.J. FitzPatrick signing the Official Twinning Agreement between Lycée Camille Sée and Ballyclare High in 1995. *(The Ballyclare High School Archive)*

Archbishop and Lady Eames with F. Bailie (Head Boy) and K. Reid (Head Girl) at the Distribution of Prizes held on the September 27th 1996. *(The Ballyclare High School Archive)*

E. Hewitt with the Speaker, Miss Betty Boothroyd.

In 1997 Elaine Hewitt, who was studying Politics in the Sixth Form, won the senior category of the Young Political Writers Award sponsored by the Hansard Society and *The Guardian*. Part of her prize was a tour of the House of Commons and a meeting with the then Speaker, Miss Betty Boothroyd. Elaine also had the opportunity to attend Prime Minister's Question Time. In the same year, Mrs June Cree was appointed to the Senior Staff.

The following year the school had great success in scientific competitions. Mark Bridgham, who was Head Boy in 1997/98, won the Irish Biology Olympiad in January, and at the British Biology Olympiad the following month five Year 14 pupils were awarded five medals, including one Gold. In July Mark Bridgham attended the International Biology Olympiad in Germany, where he was awarded a bronze medal, and in November he was awarded second prize in the Sir Hans Sloane Memorial Award for his A Level marks in Biology, Chemistry and Physics.

Whilst the new decade brought success and opportunities, it brought sadness too. Catherine Nicholl, an honours graduate of Queen's University, Belfast, joined the staff of Ballyclare High School in September 1980. She was appointed to teach Chemistry and Biology, although later specialised in Biology. Sadly, Miss Nicholl died in March 1991 and a Memorial Service for her was held on May 1st 1991. In January 1995 a former Head Girl, Roberta Weatherup, was killed in a tragic accident. Roberta had had an outstanding academic career, both at school and at University College, Oxford. The Roberta Weatherup Memorial Award was inaugurated at the Prize Distribution in September 1995. Craig McMillan, who played as a wing-forward for the 1st XV, sustained a broken neck and severe spinal injuries during the annual fixture against Ballyclare R.F.C. Under-18 XV on December 27th 1999, leaving him with a life-long physical disability. To help Craig, a massive collective effort swung into action, including the creation of the Craig McMillan Trust Fund. A great role-model, Craig returned to school the following year and completed his studies, before embarking on a degree at the University of Ulster at Jordanstown.

As the 1990s progressed, it was clear that the Preparatory Department was becoming less viable. The subvention from the Department of Education was reducing, which meant that fees would have had to increase substantially. In addition, with the criteria for admission unable to guarantee transfer to the Senior School, classes were becoming too small to provide a large enough peer group to ensure its future. The closure of the Preparatory Department in June 1998 was a defining moment in the school's first century. Many had gone from the Prep. to the Senior School and indeed beyond to teach in the school, or serve as Governors. Its demise broke a clear line of continuity with the school's infancy, but Ballyclare High was changing with changing times.

It had long been an ambition of Mr FitzPatrick to bring together the musical talent of past and present pupils. Wish became reality in March 2000, when thousands of pupils, past pupils, staff and former members of staff and others associated with Ballyclare High met for a gala concert at Belfast's Waterfront Hall.

Marianne Adams, a former pupil and Head of the Preparatory Department from 1984-98, reflects on her time at Ballyclare High School.

For people of my generation the heart of the school was the Assembly Hall. In later years I used to look around it and think about how much it reflected my years in Ballyclare High, since I entered the school as a nervous and very excited eleven year-old in 1953.

In that Assembly Hall, I had gone to my first school party, with R.E. Russell in the middle of the mêlée of Third Formers, keeping us in order with a whistle. In that Assembly Hall, I had often stepped in late by the side door when I'd overslept. In that Assembly Hall, I received my Senior Certificate and attended my first grown-up dance, known far and wide as 'The Hop', and in that Assembly Hall I had taken numerous classes, play rehearsals, and P.E. when I returned to teach in the Preparatory Department after three years at Stranmillis.

The Prep. in those days was housed all over the town in Orange and Church halls, but we always met back in the Assembly Hall for the highlight of the school year – Prep. Prize Day. Kings and Queens, elves and gnomes, wise men and angels paraded across that little stage; even after we had been housed in three rooms along the Prep. Corridor where we remained until the Department closed in June 1998.

By that time I was Head of the Prep. Department, and in the intervening years had taught every class from Primary 1-7. They were happy years for me and I hope for the children who attended the school. It was small, protective and family-orientated and I like to think is held in some affection by the pupils who started their education there.

I spent most of the years from 1953 to 1998 in Ballyclare High. I worked under four Principals and saw the school change from a small rural establishment of 450 children where everyone knew everyone else, to a large one of 1,200 pupils and 80 plus teachers, serving all of Newtownabbey and beyond. I watched walls being knocked down, rooms amalgamated to make space for computers, science labs turned into classrooms and art rooms into music suites.

The one place that remained, as I had first known it all those years ago, was the Assembly Hall and some of my happiest memories, both as pupil and teacher, are evoked by events there.

P. Coulter and A. Lyness are presented with their awards by H.R.H. the Duke of Kent at the National Final of the Young Engineers for Britain Competition in 1996. *(The Ballyclare High School Archive)*

A presentation to honour former pupil Gary Longwell's appearance in the European Cup Winning Team of 1999. *From left to right:* Mr F. Gault, P. Johnston (Captain, 1st XV), Mr B. McBride from the Bank of Ireland, G. Longwell, Mr T. Young and Mr J. Whincup. *(The Ballyclare High School Archive)*

Photographed at the presentation of Gold Duke of Edinburgh's Award Certificates at St. James' Palace, London in December 1998 are from *left to right*: P. Wylie, R. McKenzie, Mr R.J. FitzPatrick, G. Acheson, S. Stirling, J. Auld, M. Bridgham, K. Rankin, C. Duff, C. McCartney, A. Dunlop, G. Johnston, K. Caldwell, E. Crawford, Mr S.R. Moore and Mr J.M.A. Farquhar. *(The Ballyclare High School Archive)*

In the same year, David Knox was appointed Principal after Mr FitzPatrick's retirement. Mr Knox had begun his career in 1975, teaching English at Cambridge House Boys' Grammar School in Ballymena, where he became Head of English and Senior Teacher. In 1997 he became Vice-Principal at Victoria College, Belfast, with responsibility for Administration and Resources. In Mr Knox's first year at Ballyclare, the school was presented with the Enterprising School Award by the Ulster Bank, to recognise "achievement including charity work and building European and international links with other colleges".

D.A. Knox – appointed Principal in 2000. (The Ballyclare High School Archive)

Receiving the Enterprising School Award. From left: Dr R.M. McMillen, Sir George Quigley (Chairman, Ulster Bank), Mr D.A. Knox, Mrs C. Branagh and Mr R.J. Fitzpatrick. (The Ballyclare High School Archive)

Former pupil, James McIlroy, who was selected for the Great Britain Athletics Team (800m) for the 2000 Sydney Olympics presenting his G.B. vest to Mr Knox. The staff involved in the coaching of athletics are back left: Mr J. Whincup, Mr J. Dougan, Mr T. Young, Mr J. Rafferty and Mr W. Hollinger. (The Ballyclare High School Archive)

Musically, the school has had a strong reputation for decades. When it was written that "the song singing is inclined to be rather lifeless whilst the tone is not all that is to be desired", it was certainly not applicable to the Chamber Choir in the 1990s under the leadership of John Dallas and Sam Moreland. It actually comes from an inspector's report from the late 1940s! The Choir have achieved consistent success in the UTV Choir of the Year Competition from the mid-1990s. The Wind Band came second in the Northern Ireland Wind Band competition in October 2002. Many who attended the school and participated in its many musical activities have achieved notable success in their careers. For example, Joe McKee, a former Head Boy, is now Head of the City of Belfast School of Music and Colin Fleming is the Principal Flautist of the Ulster Orchestra. Sheelagh Greer is a full-time musician and has won numerous awards for vocal performance at music festivals throughout Northern Ireland.

The highly successful Chamber Choir 1999/2000

Back left: S. Stewart, T. Coburn, D. Hume, S. McCullough, A. Cooper, G. Davidson, J. Caldwell, D. Arthur, A. Houston, and G. English. *Middle left:* Mr J.R. Dallas, V. Moreland, D. Caldwell, V. Booth, V. Hamilton, A. Clarke, R. Crawford, M. Moreland, S. Robinson, S. Tang, E. Jacks, C. Hamilton, V. Burrell and Mr S. Moreland. *Front left:* A. Agnew, A. Morgan, H. Malcomson, R. McKendry, C. Magee, P. Campbell, C. Martin, J. Young and D. Currie. *(The Ballyclare High School Archive)*

In 2002 the school was again awarded the prestigious International School Award. This award, granted by the British Council, had been awarded to Ballyclare High School in 1999, in recognition of its formal and informal curriculum having a significant international element. The year also brought the retirement of Mr James Rafferty, Head of Art, who had been with the school for over three decades. At his retirement function many speakers noted how he had been instrumental in putting the school 'on the map' in Irish school athletics. Notably, Mr Wilbert Hollinger, who first represented Ireland in orienteering at the World Championships in 1976, had received the prestigious Nestlé Tailteann 'Ideal' Merit Award in 1998 for his "outstanding contribution to Irish Schools' Athletics".

Pictured at the opening of the 'Sam Bell Laboratories' and the inauguration of the ICT network in 1999 are *back left*: Mr S. Bell and Mr G. Topping (Chief Executive, NEELB). *Front row*: R. Herron, D. Curry and R. Skillen. *(The Ballyclare High School Archive)*

This photograph is from the Pakistan Expedition that took place in June and July 2001 organised by World Challenge Expeditions. The company offers the opportunity for teams of young people to plan a month long trip to a developing country, during which time they complete a demanding trek and take part in a community project. The aim is to develop teamwork amongst the students alongside adventure, discovery and challenge. This photograph was taken early in the expedition just off the Karakorum Highway on the way from Islamabad to Karimabad in the Hunza Valley in northern Pakistan. It is at the junction of the three highest mountain ranges: the Hindukush, the Karakorum and the Himalayas. *Left:* P. Moore, A. Wilson, Mr J. Whincup, S. Canavan, T. Coburn, P. Stirling, P. Morris, E. Hughes, J. Lutton, C. Crawford, M. Ashcroft, K. Neill, A. Kelly, N. Robinson and R. Moore. This photograph was taken by Mr W. Hollinger.

Resourcing teaching and learning is a perennial problem in education.

It is now ten years since we first started Computer Studies in Ballyclare High School. We continually hear the moans from the rapidly growing bunch of enthusiasts: if only we had another machine. (Richard Wallace, 1983).

Since then the school has made phenomenal progress in the whole area of ICT. This growth spans the Headships of Mr Millar, Mr FitzPatrick and the current Headmaster Mr Knox, all of whom have played their part in ICT gaining such prominence in Ballyclare High. From the pioneering days of using 380Z computers, through the frustrations of using BBC computers and the Apple Mac adventure, it has been quite a pilgrimage of enterprise. Rooms 124 and 125 have been refurbished three times in the past 17 years, to ensure that an effective ICT network of computers could support teaching and learning. The opening of the school's new network, based on a PC platform, was further enhanced by the introduction of new intellidesk computers in 2003, to place Ballyclare High in the forefront of ICT innovation in the Province. The use of Open Access areas has promoted independence in pupils' learning and the development of cluster groups in a range of areas throughout the school has promoted innovation in teaching. Others who visited the school and noted the significant impact of ICT on pupils and teachers alike have duplicated these developments.

The development of a most effective whole-school intranet and an extensive internet site, now in its second edition, has attracted acclaim from visitors to the ICT provision within the school. In February 2002 the school won the prestigious Gold Award at the Institute of IT Training Awards at the Dorchester Hotel in London. Mr Richard Wallace won the Becta Manager of the Year Award and further success came later in the year when Ballyclare High became a Laureate School for its innovative and effective use of

Educational Technology. Such is the state of excitement in the school that almost certainly this marks the beginning of a whole new era of expectancy about how ICT can be used by the next generation of pupils and teachers.

As the school's first century was drawing to a close, badminton had probably its most successful year when the Minor Boys' team won the 2003 Ulster Minor Boys' Cup, the League, and the All-Ireland Championships. This was the first time in the school's history that a team of boys had won three such titles in one year. Table Tennis also brought honour to the school when teams won the Under 14 Trophy and the Junior Cup. Rugby had its successes too. The Medallion XV completed a highly successful season by winning the Plate Competition at Ravenhill. They defeated Portora Royal School in the Final, having already secured comfortable

Vice-Principal Mr R. Wallace receiving the 'Manager of the Year Award' from Baroness Ashford and Professor T. Wragg at the Becta 2002 Ceremony in London. *(R. Wallace Collection)*

Some of those who participated in the Debating Society's Ulster-Scots debate in 2002. *Left to right:* M. McLean, Lord Laird of Artigarvan, Mr L. Reid, G. Barton, and Mr D. Kennedy. *(The Ballyclare High School Archive)*

As noted earlier, Drama has played an important role throughout the school's history, but in more recent times there has been a widening in the opportunities available. In 2002 ten girls from the school teamed up with Dominican College to perform *Very Aggressive Hats*, a play about the suffragette movement in Ulster. This was performed at the Island Hill Arts Centre, Lisburn, and pupils have also performed at other venues such as the Waterfront Hall and Ballyearl Arts Centre.

In more recent years the school has forged ahead in the teaching of Citizenship and has become one of the leading schools in the Province for providing pupils with the opportunity to engage in civic and community links. Although Citizenship has been much promoted in education in the last decade, it has actually enjoyed a long tradition in Ballyclare High School. Edie Laird, who retired from teaching in 1972, took the importance of 'Good Citizenship' as her theme when Guest Speaker at the Prize Distribution in that year. The school now has a teacher who coordinates Citizenship and it is integrated into not just the formal curriculum, but also Personal, Social and Health Education.

victories over Carrickfergus Grammar, Belfast High School and Grosvenor Grammar. In the summer of 2003 the 1st XV had another highly successful tour of Canada, building on the experience of previous tours to Russia, Italy and Canada. The 1st XI, captained by Stefanie McGowan, had toured Canada in August 1992 and it was during this decade that sporting tours became much more common and many former pupils look back fondly on their experiences as pupils abroad.

Winners of the All Ireland Minor Boys' Badminton Championship 2003. *Left to right:* M. Lynch, P. Ross, A. Shannon (Captain) and J. Hanley. *(E. McKinney)*

C. McAllister (Oberon) and S. Starrett (Titania) from the production of *A Midsummer Night's Dream* staged in the Millennium Garden in June 2002. The piece was adapted and directed by Mrs C. Thompson from the English Department.

The victorious Medallion team that won the Plate Competition in 2003

Back left: C. Abernethy, A. McCullough, R. Hackney, A. Johnson, S. Cusick and Mr G. Lenaghan. *Middle left:* Mr J. Whincup, A. Kirk, G. Glendenning, R. McConnell, W. Goulden, G. Jeffrey, W. Stewart and Mr G. Shaw. *Front left:* J. Jackson, P. Robinson, M. Holmes, R. Wilson (Captain), R. Logan, A. McQuoid and J. Reid.
(D. Douglas)

The School Aid Romania Team 2003. *Back left:* L. Stewart, Miss J. Dickey, C. Dickey, Mr M. Dickie, H. Gamble, J. Heaney and V. Clintock. *Middle left:* S. Boyd, G. Spiers, R. Mairs, E. Peoples and T. Smith. *Front left:* B. Behzadafshar, P. Stirling, E. McCallion and R. Buckley. *(The Ballyclare High School Archive)*

Three Principals. Mr D.A. Knox (standing) with Mr G.C.G. Millar (1971-1990) and Mr R.J. FitzPatrick (1990-2000). *(T. Martin)*

Amy Blair was a Year 8 pupil at the time of the Centenary Concert in the Waterfront Hall, Belfast. Perhaps reflecting both the change and continuity with the past, this is how she viewed the school as a first form pupil in 2003.

B.H.S. is a great place to be. Despite all the work, I really enjoy the social aspect of life here. My mum used to go to the school and was Head Girl in 1977/78 and took part in operas such as *Ruddigore*, *The Mikado* and *H.M.S. Pinafore*. My sister also goes to the school and is in year 12 doing her GCSEs. Scary!

The school canteen. Now there's something I wasn't expecting when I first came to the school. The constant roar of the crowd when somebody drops something; the never-to-be-got-to-the-end-of-in-time queues all come to make the canteen a place I try to avoid at all costs. Thinking of which, £1.50 for a curried chip!

I wasn't really prepared for the number of people or the size of the school either. My first day had to be the scariest. Seeing all the Sixth Year boys and girls walking around the corridors waiting to give you lines was the worst but I think I'm getting used to that now and I am staying on the right side of these 'respected' members of our school!

When the bell rings in the morning, there is the usual stampede for the doors, causing major traffic jams at all the entrances. Then, when you've recovered from that, you have the task of trying to work out which room you are in for your next lesson.

When I look back on my primary school days, I remember the few old second-hand computers in one half of my P6 teacher's room. Bless! We at Ballyclare High are very lucky to have a vast amount of equipment for everyday use.

I enjoy my time at B.H.S. I have a great laugh with my friends, including some teachers, and I hope I do well in my exams too.

The Board of Governors 2003

Back left: Mr K. Canavan, Dr A. Millar, Mr A. McKinstry, Mr K. Lindsay, Rev. P. Campbell, Mr T. Douglas and Mr J. Blayney. *Front left:* Mrs J. Allen, Mr C. Steele, Mrs C. Coburn (Vice-Chairman), Dr R. McMillen (Chairman), Mr D. Knox (Principal), Mr H. Mawhinney, Mrs B. Acheson and Mrs R. Moore. *Not present:* Alderman V. McWilliam and Mr M. Johnston. *(W. Mateer)*

The Staff 2003

Back left: T. Young, T. Thomlinson, M. Farquhar, S. Black, M. Rainey, H. Graham, P. Leckey, R. Milliken, M. Dickie, L. Reid, J. Dallas, R. Shields, K. Conway, C. Waring, F. Gault, J. Whincup and J. Moffett. *Second row from back. Left:* S. McClements, M. Nutt, G. Scott, W. Loughrey, V. Johnston, G. Morrison, J. Currie, A. Heaney, E. Walker, A. Strange, J. Anderson, J. Dickey, A. Millar, V. Adamson, B. Griffith, M. Farley, E. Coon, T. Walsh, C. Thompson and N. Blayney. *Middle left:* R. Shearer, E. McConnell, A. Ritchie, J. Fullerton, A. Brunet, G. Renard, R. McKee, D. McMillan, M. McKeown, L. Gilmour, F. Moore, S. Duke, L. Nelson, H. Wynn, C. Courtney, A. Spence, S. Brown, C. McGaffin, J. Maxwell and S. Edgar. *Front left:* D. Campbell, A. Wilson, S. Moreland, C. Branagh, J. Scott, J. Cree, J. Dougan, W. Hollinger, D. Knox (Principal), M. Stewart, T. Martin, R. Acheson, B. Dyer, R. Moore, P. Reid, T. Stewart and E. McKinney. *Not present:* R. Wallace, A. Kennedy, K. Orr, G. Lenaghan, J. Adamson, T. Coleman, N. Browne, J. Gaston, J. Thomson, P. McKeown, H. Lynn, J. Ross and S. Moore. *(W. Mateer)*

In June 2001 School Councils were introduced at Junior, Intermediate and Senior level, to give pupils of all ages the opportunity actively to experiment with democratic participation. This has led to environmental improvements within the school, which have in turn assisted Ballyclare High School's success in being placed in the Shell Best Kept School Awards for the past three years. Utilising new computer conferencing technology, some classes have taken part in Distance Learning Citizenship Projects with the University of Ulster at Coleraine. In 2002 the school hosted the Junior Mock United Nations General Assembly that brought together Year 10 pupils from Ballyclare High, Rostulla Special School, Newtownabbey, St. Dominic's High School, Belfast, and Victoria College, Belfast.

In June and July 2003 two Sixth Form students, Carlo Eastwood and Lauren Gilroy, represented Ballyclare High School and the United Kingdom at a Global Young Leaders' Conference in Washington D.C. and New York. Three hundred and fifty students attended the conference that explored international politics, finance, law, culture and diplomacy with key policy makers. Delegates visited a range of institutions such as the World Bank, the United States Department of State and the United Nations.

As Ballyclare High School entered its Centenary year, Mr Knox reflected on the school's past and recorded how he views the changes and challenges of the twenty-first century affecting this long-established Grammar School in County Antrim:

The history of Ballyclare High School is the story of its progress and achievements as it has developed and changed to meet the needs of its pupils and their community. It is the story of a school that has encouraged enterprise, effort and adventure over the years. In days gone by, when accommodation and resources were much more sparse than they are today, the spirit of those who were involved in taking the school forward was undaunted. They showed pride and a sense of purpose in the work they were doing and their confidence was transferred from one generation of pupils to the next through a common bond of comradeship.

As we look to the future, it is with hope and determination that the school will retain that spirit and remain worthy of the reputation it has gained, earning continuing respect for its accomplishments. The enduring mixture of traditional and progressive, of old and new, of rural and urban, is one of the great strengths of this institution.

The sight of teachers wearing traditional academic gowns while demonstrating the latest in educational technology leads sometimes to wry smiles from our visitors. But that is how we are, proudly contradictory; conservative and traditional, yet embracing the new and the modern when it suits us to do so. It is a credit to the staff of the school that they have moved forward together, showing enthusiasm to master the skills and the changes in mindset that are required purposefully to integrate new approaches and teaching and learning techniques. It was appropriate that, on November 24th 2003, Ballyclare High School was chosen as one of only four schools in the United Kingdom to meet the Fathers of the Internet, Bob Kahn and Vint Cerf, to discuss with them the impact of their world-transforming invention. The video-conference was entitled "The Fathers of the Internet meet the Children of the Internet".

Much space has been devoted in this volume to the story of the buildings of the school. Now, in 2004, we are looking forward once more to the completion of a new extension, comprising three new ICT classrooms and a new Library/Information Centre. This will give the School the additional capacity that it needs to meet the ever-growing demand for resources and to expand opportunities for independent learning. These facilities, when added to our already refurbished network rooms, and our planned new network, will match any in Northern Ireland. I have great confidence that the staff will maximise the use of these impressive resources.

But we can never be complacent. Our goal is to work confidently to improve the educational provision that we offer. Increasingly, I believe we are showing a willingness to be self-critical and evaluative. We are becoming more adept at gathering evidence from our pupils and parents and from our results to measure our performance, to take stock of what we are achieving and to identify targets for the future. Of course this is not an end itself, but a means to improve the quality of our teaching and learning and to improve the standards that our pupils attain. We are willing to accept criticism as well as praise in order to improve the quality of the service we provide.

Nowhere is that service more impressive than in the musical performances over the years that have enhanced the reputation of the school so much. There can be few schools that offer a richer and more varied programme than that manifested recently in our Centenary Concert. Through our light opera productions, our choirs, orchestra, wind band and various instrumental ensembles the school expresses itself imaginatively and creatively on public occasions. And I hope that increasingly through dance and drama we will extend the repertoire. How dull and dreary any school would be without such opportunities for its talent to be enjoyed and shared.

In recent years Ballyclare High has been involved in international links with a number of European Schools. Contacts are still maintained through exchange visits with Lycée Camille Sée, Colmar Alsace in France and Gymnasium Petrinum, Dorsten in Germany. Through the Comenius Project 1, in 1997, Ballyclare High School helped to design and manufacture a component of a roboarm. At a further Comenius conference in Belfast, hosted by the North Eastern Education and Library Board in November 2002, project planning resulted in a successful application for funding to Socrates Agencies and this has led to partnership with three schools, IES General Alemon, Ronda in Spain, Gymnasium Peitz, Brandenberg in Germany and Collège Lucion Gahot, Auvergne in France. This project will link together a number of subjects on the curriculum.

Since 1999 Ballyclare High has worked with schools in Brandenberg and Berlin to promote international mini-enterprise by pupils. Teamwork and transferable life-long skills have been developed through working with our Partner Schools. I believe that this international aspect of our work will expand even further in the future as we focus on global citizenship issues and extend the range of schools with which we have links.

Citizenship, currently being developed through our Life Skills programme, focuses on the Themes of Diversity, Human Rights and Democracy. Pupils have undertaken a video-conferencing link with students taking the Post Graduate Certificate in Education Programme at the University of Ulster, Coleraine. We have also worked with schools in the Republic of Ireland on a Civic Link Programme. Recently, a School Council site was launched on our Intranet to communicate to all pupils the work that their elected representatives do in putting across their views and interests to the Senior Management of the School as well as to the Board of Governors, whom they meet annually.

The steps that have already been taken to broaden the curriculum and to increase its relevance as a preparation for adult life are, I believe, the beginning of a sustained reorganisation of the curriculum that will take place over the next decade. At the time of writing, internal discussions have already begun on the proposals for a new curriculum at Key Stage 3. It seems likely that in the future subjects will work together much more closely to ensure that pupils can more easily make links and connections between them. It also seems likely that in the reorganisation of the curriculum we may look for opportunities to escape from the constraints of the traditional timetable to create broader learning opportunities for our pupils. This shift from compartmentalised learning to a more integrated approach will occupy the attentions of our staff from 2005 onwards, as they review the content of their teaching, but we must ensure that it will not result in any diminution of the integrity and rigour of our subjects. That would

be a retrograde step. I have confidence that common sense will prevail at Ballyclare High School and that we will still strike that balance between the traditional and the progressive that has been the hallmark of this school over many years.

The centenary celebrations began with a concert in the Waterfront Hall, Belfast, in April 2003. This photograph shows the choirs, orchestra and dancers conducted by Mr S. Moreland, perform extracts from *Carmina Burana. (T. Martin)*

Principals	Vice-Principals	Chairmen of the Board of Governors
Miss C. Aikin	Mr J.K. Elliott	Rev. W. Brann
Mr A. Fowweather	Mr T.J. Davidson	Rev. J. Armstrong
Mr R.E. Russell	Mr H.A. Mudd	Mr A. McConnell
Mr J.D. Williams	Mr L. Francey	Rev. W.J.G. Macbeth
Mr H.A. Mudd *(Acting Principal)*	Mr R. Thornbury	Rev. W. Hall
Mr G.C.G. Millar	Mr S.M. Bell	Mr J.H. Lindsay M.B.E.
Mr R.J. FitzPatrick	Miss M.P. Stewart	Mrs R. Moore
Mr D.A. Knox	Mr W.R. Hollinger	Mr S.R. Cameron
	Mr R. Wallace	Mr C.H. Mawhinney
		Dr R.M. McMillen

Head Boy and Head Girl, R. Campbell and M. Hassard, as The Mikado and Katisha from *The Mikado* performed in October 2003. *(T. Martin)*

From left: Dr. and Mrs R. McMillen, Professor and Mrs A. McClean and Mr and Mrs D. Knox. *(Newtownabbey Times,* 3rd October 2003)

Professor Emeritus Albert J. McClean, a former Head Boy, was the guest speaker at the Centenary Prize Distribution in September 2003. In the course of his address, Professor McClean recalled:

As you have heard I started in Kilbride, a small elementary country school. I thoroughly enjoyed what I did there, but if you had asked me how good the education was I had no basis on which to make a judgement.

In a sense, the first test of that education was when I transferred here to the High School. What I found was that that little country school had given me a superb foundation for what I was expected to do here. In due course I found that what I did here provided a superb foundation for what I did at Queen's, Cambridge and Michigan. Throughout my career, I have had the good fortune to rub shoulders with university colleagues, students, lawyers, business people, who had attended schools, some with stellar reputations, in all parts of the world, and I have always felt, indeed been confident, that my education at Kilbride and Ballyclare held its own with the best of them.

So a little school which started in a minor way a hundred years ago by my time, the 1950s, provided a first class education. The impression I have, on this too long delayed return, is that in the last 50 years it has simply gone from strength to strength and stands poised to continue that development.

Conclusion

No school's history is ever truly complete. As historians know only too well, it is usually during the final stages of publication or even afterwards that some new information, reminiscence, photograph or other gem appears. This of course comes with the territory, but is nonetheless immensely frustrating. Those with an interest in the school will always have their own memories and recollections. However, many Old Ballyclarians from different generations identify candidly the tangibly distinctive spirit and ethos of the school: perhaps it is the shared experience of education, or the multiplicity of challenges that the school and its stakeholders, be they staff or pupils, have encountered over its first century of achievement. Nevertheless, the indomitable spirit of the staff and pupils over the span of its existence provides a unifying thread of continuity from the Aikin era to the school in the early twenty-first century.

Historically, the school has weathered numerous storms of educational change and uncertainty. For some, it was the difficulties in keeping the school a viable proposition in its very early years before it moved to the North End of the town in 1916. Miss Aikin had also to embrace whole-scale change in the governance of her school in the years immediately following Partition. For a later generation, it was the educational revolution of the 1947 Education Act that introduced selection. Yet even in the first half-century, we can see clearly the leaders of the school embracing change and recognising that it also brought opportunities. At the Prize Distribution in 1948, Mr Russell noted that the Act enabled "teachers and parents to provide a better and fuller education, and the means of enjoying a better life for the rising generation". Similarly, Mr Knox, in his address at the Prize Distribution in 2003, noted that "teachers have been embracing the new technologies and recognising the new challenges". He added that even "as the school adjusts to the technological, educational and social changes of the new century, the core values of Ballyclare High School, are still wholeheartedly expressed in *Industria et Probitate*".

If the continuities between the past and the present are clear there are also vast differences. Inevitably, the curriculum has been revised and expanded, as has the nature of external examinations. In the school's second half-century, a much greater proportion of its pupils secured places in higher education. As academic standards were maintained, many pupils brought a plethora of honours to the school. Moreover, the school has gone from surviving with very rudimentary facilities in its early years to being well-resourced, over-subscribed and a leader amongst Northern Ireland's finest schools in its use of Information Technology.

When one considers the role that Ballyclare High has played in the local, wider and international community over its first one hundred years, we begin to get an idea of the tremendous debt of gratitude owed to the early pioneers who had to overcome so many difficulties. Conceivably, one of the greatest tributes is that vast numbers of parents over the generations have sent their children to what was once their own school and have actively supported its consistent efforts in so many ways, such as involvement with the Parent Teacher Association. Undoubtedly, the diaspora of the school stretches across the globe, encompassing a vast diversity of professions and occupations. Perhaps, though, what matters more is the experience of those who went through Ballyclare High School and their memories of it.

Mrs A. McMullan, who at 105 years of age, is the school's oldest past pupil. (*The Ballyclare High School Archive*)

Acknowledgements

Historians are often parasitic when it comes to securing the help of others. I would like to thank the members of the Centenary Committee, Dr R. McMillen, Mr D. Knox, Mr G. Nutt, Mr K. Canavan and Mrs J. Allen, for their advice and assistance throughout the duration of this project. Many read the manuscript, either in whole or in part, and I thank them all for their assistance, although of course I accept responsibility for any errors.

There really are far too many people to thank individually, but the following were a great help:

Miss M. Adams, Mr T. Andrew, Mr M. Armour, Mr A. Bowden, Mrs C. Branagh, Mrs A. Brown, Mr N. Browne, Mrs N. Caldwell, Mr D. Campbell, Mrs C. Courtney, Mrs J. Cree, Mr J. Dallas, Mr J. Dougan, Mr D. Douglas, Mrs V. Douglas, Mrs S. Duke, Dr E. Dunlop, Mrs B. Dyer, Mr M. Farley, Mr M. Farquhar, Mr R. FitzPatrick, Mr F. Gault, Mr B. Griffith, Mr R. Hassard, Mr D. Hawthorne, Mrs L. Heaton, Mrs J. Holland, Mr W. Hollinger, Mrs Y. Hirst, Mrs J. Jenkins, Miss V. Johnson, Mr E. Laird, Mr G. Lenaghan, Miss E. McConnell, Mrs L. McCullough, Mrs M. McGuigan, Mr R. McKay, Mr E. McKinney, Mr J. McKinney, Mrs S. McKinney, Mrs A. McMullan, Mrs S. Mairs, Mr T. Martin, Mr W. Mateer, Mr J. Maxwell, Mr C. Millar, Mrs R. Moore, Mr S. Moreland, Mrs L. Nelson, Mr T. Noble, Mr A. Powers, Mr A. Reid, Mr L. Reid, Miss A. Ritchie, Mr K. Robinson, Miss J. Scott, Mr R. Shields, Mrs F. Stevenson, Miss M. Stewart, Mr S. Stewart, Mr T. Stewart, Mrs C. Thompson, Mr S. Thompson, Ms J. Thomson, Mr B. Tipping, Mr R. Wallace, Mr C. Waring, Mrs B. Whincup, Mr J. Whincup, Mr A. Wilson, Mr J. Wilson, Mr T. Young and the 'IT Dept. from 10B' 2002/03.

Many institutions provided assistance but the following were particularly helpful: Ballyclare Library, Larne Library, Carrickfergus Library, Ballymena Library, the Local Studies Department at Ballymena, the Ulster Folk and Transport Museum and the Public Record Office of Northern Ireland.

Photographs and inserts

Credit has been given, where possible, for the photographs reproduced throughout the book. Many credited to the Ballyclare High School Archive have been handed into the school over a number of decades and it has been virtually impossible to trace their origins. However, I wish to record my thanks to all of those who supplied photographs and background information. Thanks also to the *News Letter, Down Recorder, Ballymena Times and Ballymena Observer, Larne Times, Newtownabbey Times* and the Deputy Keeper of the Records, Public Record Office of Northern Ireland for their permission to reproduce both photographic and written material.

Select Bibliography

Much of the information contained within this book is a result of numerous interviews conducted over the past three years. In addition to a large range of official school documentation, such as Governors' minutes, magazines and correspondence, the following were very useful:

E. Laird, Some Thoughts on the Origins and Development of Ballyclare High School – Unpublished Manuscript.

A. Fowweather, *One Small Head* (Downpatrick, 1980).

F.M. McDowell, *Other Days Around Me* (Belfast, 1966).

J. McKinney, *Where the Six Mile Water Flows* (Belfast, 1991).